101 Things You
Wish You'd Invented

... and Some You Wish No One Had

D0711357

* Write your own dedications in here

Richard dedicates this book to

Helen *

Tracey dedicates this book to

Toby *

First published in Great Britain in 2008

Bloomsbury Publishing Plc, 36 Soho Square, London, W1D 3QY

Copyright © 2008 by Richard Horne and Tracey Turner

The moral rights of the authors/illustrator have been asserted

All rights reserved
No part of this publication may be reproduced or transmitted
by any means, electronic, mechanical, photocopying
or otherwise, without the prior permission of the publisher

A CIP catalogue record for this book is available from the British Library

ISBN 978 0 7475 9198 6

1 3 5 7 9 10 8 6 4 2

Printed in Malaysia by Tien Wah Press

All papers used by Bloomsbury Publishing are natural, recyclable products
made from wood grown in well-managed forests. The manufacturing
processes conform to the environmental regulations of the country of origin.

www.101thingstodo.co.uk
www.bloomsbury.com

101 Things You Wish You'd Invented
...and Some You Wish No One Had

Write your name here

Designed and illustrated by Richard Horne
Written by Tracey Turner and Richard Horne

BLOOMSBURY

Introduction

Ever wondered how a lie detector works? Or how a thermometer measures the temperature? Why we need time zones, or why some people thought nuclear weapons were a good idea? The world is full of incredible **Inventions** (and some not so good ones), far too many to learn about them all, so here are 101 of the cleverest, weirdest and best.

Discover

Learn how the visually impaired read, how to make your own mini hot-air balloon, how to terraform a planet and what 'dit' and 'dot' mean. The answers lie inside, so sharpen your curiosity – and prepare to be amazed ...

Complete

Keep track of the **Inventions** you have explored by filling in the easy-to-follow forms.

Bask in the Glory

When you have finished, you will have developed a keen, enquiring and, most importantly, inventive mind to rival Leonardo himself.

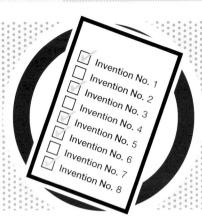

How to Use This Book

The idea is simple. Master the **101 Things You Wish You'd Invented and Some You Wish No One Had**, tick the boxes, fill in the forms and stick in the coloured stars as you go.

About the Forms

- Be honest with the information you enter in the forms.
- There may be a few tricky questions on some of the forms. Don't worry if you get stuck – you'll find the answers at the back of the book.
- You may find some of the forms too small for all the information you'd like to enter. To solve this problem you can copy the extra pages at the back of the book or visit the website for extra or duplicate pages at **www.101thingstodo.co.uk**.

Your **Inventions**

If there are some **Inventions** which aren't mentioned in the book, add your top ten **Inventions** on the pages provided at the back.

Helpful Tips

The tips on the opposite page offer some guidelines to completing the **Things You Wish You'd Invented**.

101 Things You Wish You'd Invented
and Some You Wish No One Had

Tips

✔ Master as many **Inventions** as possible and fill in your results in the book as you go along.

✔ Always carry this book with you to dazzle anyone and everyone with amazing **Invention** facts.

✔ As you learn about more amazing **Inventions**, be aware that friends may envy how interesting and knowledgeable you've become.

✔ You don't have to go it alone. Many of the **Inventions** will be more fun if you master them with the help of your friends (and stop them being envious too).

✔ Push yourself. This book is crammed with fascinating **Inventions**, but there's always more to discover.

✔ Think outside the box. If you find that some **Inventions** really interest you, don't stop here – do your own research and find out even more.

✔ Above all, have fun. The **Inventions** are listed to enhance your daily life and make the world more interesting.

101 Things You Wish You'd Invented
and Some You Wish No One Had

Some Things You Will Need

Here is a list of some of the items you will need to complete
the **101 Things You Wish You'd Invented and Some You Wish
No One Had**. You don't need to have them all before you start,
but it's advisable to at least have a pen, a pair of scissors,
glue, a camera, access to a computer and some money. You
can get hold of the other items as you continue through the
list, but the willingness to learn, a sense of adventure,
spontaneity, a mischievous spirit, a sense of humour, a good
imagination and optimism are all down to you.

- ☐ A secret hiding place for this book!
- ☐ A brain like a sponge
- ☐ A good imagination
- ☐ Neat handwriting
- ☐ A pen
- ☐ Paper
- ☐ Glue
- ☐ A camera
- ☐ A computer
- ☐ A photocopier
- ☐ A pair of scissors
- ☐ Some empty bottles
- ☐ A little help from your parents
- ☐ A little help from your friends
- ☐ A yo-yo
- ☐ The Sun
- ☐ The Moon
- ☐ The stars
- ☐ A lemon
- ☐ A nail
- ☐ Some coins
- ☐ Many types of tea
- ☐ Lots of blank space on your body for tattoos
- ☐ Tissue paper
- ☐ Some tin cans
- ☐ Playing cards
- ☐ Make-up in various colours
- ☐ Various types of old clothes
- ☐ A pair of tights
- ☐ Salt
- ☐ Water
- ☐ A pair of old jeans
- ☐ A banana
- ☐ A needle
- ☐ Some great music
- ☐ Dance moves
- ☐ A rock stance
- ☐ An invisible guitar
- ☐ A suspicious mind
- ☐ A handkerchief
- ☐ Various satellites
- ☐ Some matches
- ☐ Soap
- ☐ A refrigerator
- ☐ A big bag
- ☐ A potato
- ☐ A skateboard
- ☐ A parachute
- ☐ Post-it notes
- ☐ A football
- ☐ A roller coaster
- ☐ A strong stomach
- ☐ A paper clip
- ☐ Various pencils
- ☐ Citric acid
- ☐ Bicarbonate of soda
- ☐ A calculator
- ☐ Vinyl records
- ☐ Basic cooking skills
- ☐ A lying tongue
- ☐ A set of scales
- ☐ A cork
- ☐ A magnet
- ☐ A mobile phone
- ☐ A doppelgänger
- ☐ A sense of humour

101 Things You Wish You'd Invented
and Some You Wish No One Had

Important Information

WARNING:

WHEN EMBARKING ON THE **101 THINGS YOU WISH YOU'D INVENTED AND SOME YOU WISH NO ONE HAD** PLEASE PROCEED WITH CARE.

FOR SOME OF THE ACTIVITIES YOU WILL NEED THE SUPERVISION OF AN ADULT. IF IN DOUBT, CONSULT AN ADULT ANYWAY.

THE AUTHORS AND PUBLISHER ACCEPT NO RESPONSIBILITY FOR ANY ACCIDENTS THAT OCCUR AS A RESULT OF USING THIS BOOK.

101 Things You Wish You'd Invented
and Some You Wish No One Had

The List

1. ☐ Time	27. ☐ Pizza
2. ☐ Mobile Phone	28. ☐ Lie Detector
3. ☐ Matches	29. ☐ Post-It Notes
4. ☐ Cloning	30. ☐ Magic
5. ☐ Fast Food	31. ☐ Compass
6. ☐ Photography	32. ☐ Cutlery
7. ☐ Time Zones	33. ☐ Battery
8. ☐ Nuclear Weapons	34. ☐ Teleporter
9. ☐ Money	35. ☐ CDs and DVDs
10. ☐ Time Machine	36. ☐ Bow and Arrow
11. ☐ Fingerprinting	37. ☐ Fashion
12. ☐ Dynamite	38. ☐ Sign Language
13. ☐ Satellite	39. ☐ Toilets and Toilet Paper
14. ☐ Playing Cards	40. ☐ Spectacles
15. ☐ Tattoo	41. ☐ Football
16. ☐ Pencils	42. ☐ School
17. ☐ Morse Code	43. ☐ Sliced Bread
18. ☐ Fizzy Drinks	44. ☐ Helicopter
19. ☐ Birthdays	45. ☐ Jeans
20. ☐ Thermometer	46. ☐ Music
21. ☐ Guitar	47. ☐ Radar
22. ☐ Prison	48. ☐ Aspirin
23. ☐ Plastic	49. ☐ Homework Machine
24. ☐ Hot-Air Balloon	50. ☐ Printing
25. ☐ Poetry	51. ☐ Make-up
26. ☐ Submarine	52. ☐ Language

101 Things You Wish You'd Invented
and Some You Wish No One Had

The List

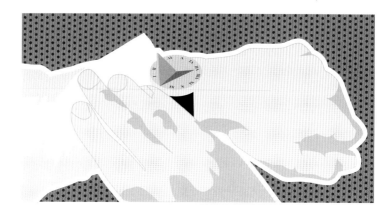

Time

Far back in the mists of ... er ... time, people must have got fed up with everyone being late for everything. Someone came up with the bright idea of time and how to measure it.

Second Nature

- The most obvious way of measuring time is, of course, the Sun coming up, going down and then coming up again: a day. People probably caught on to that one fairly fast. And the Moon goes through phases, from a sliver to a circle, of about a month, which divides time into bigger chunks.
- The Ancient Egyptians came up with the 365-day calendar. They'd noticed that some things happened once every twelve months, like the flooding of the River Nile. The earliest recorded year was 4236 BC.
- If you want to be a bit more specific, you need to divide up the day into smaller chunks. The ancient Babylonians came up with 60 seconds in a minute, 60 minutes in an hour and 24 hours in a day. Ever since then, people have been inventing time-measuring devices: clocks.

> **Clocking Off**
>
> Sundials were used to measure time over 5,000 years ago.
>
> Water clocks, which drip water at a constant rate, told the time in Egypt and Babylon around 3,500 years ago.
>
> Dutch scientist Christiaan Huygens invented the first mechanical pendulum clock in 1656.
>
> In the 20th century mechanical clocks were replaced by quartz-crystal clocks, in which crystals vibrate at a constant rate.
>
> Atomic clocks use the resonance of atoms to measure time. The first accurate one was built by Louis Essen in 1955. But not many people need to be that precise.

 Lunar-ticks: Sticks and bones with lines and holes scratched into them dating from 20,000 years ago are thought to be Ice-Age Moon calendars. Notches carved into the sticks are thought to represent days between each phase of the Moon.

Time **Form**

Once you have put this **Invention** to good use,
stick your Achieved Star here and fill in the form

Achieved

IT'S ABOUT TIME

You can't see it, hear it or stop it, but time rules our lives. With the help of the sums below,
try to work out how long you've been alive in centuries, decades, years, months, weeks,
days, hours, minutes and seconds!

1 year is equal to:
12 months • 52 weeks • 365 days • 8,760 hours
525,600 minutes • 31,536,000 seconds

10 years is equal to:
1 decade • 120 months
520 weeks • 3,650 days • 87,600 hours
5,256,000 minutes • 315,360,000 seconds

100 years is equal to:
1 century • 10 decades • 1,200 months
5,200 weeks • 36,500 days • 876,000 hours
52,560,000 minutes • 3,153,600,000 seconds

BUT these sums don't include leap years.
A leap year consists of 366 days instead of 365.
This extra day is added to February every four
years, giving the month 29 days instead of 28.

The last 10 leap years were in: 1972, 1776, 1980,
1984, 1988, 1992, 1996, 2000, 2004 & 2008.

The next 10 leap years are in: 2012, 2016,
2020, 2024, 2028, 2032, 2036, 2040, 2044 & 2048.

So for every four years that you've been alive, add:
1 day • 24 hours • 1,440 minutes • 86,400 seconds

AND if that isn't enough to think about there are
also leap seconds! Believe it or not but some
years are longer than others! Every now and again
scientists add an extra second to the year (and
sometimes two in a year). There have been 23 leap
seconds in the last 35 years. The last leap second
to be added was to the end of 31 December 2005,
making the time 23:59:60 – so bung a few extra
seconds on to your answers for good measure!

HOW LONG HAVE YOU BEEN ALIVE?

Firstly, write down ...

your birth date   today's date   the exact time NOW

hours   mins   secs

NOW DO THE MATHS

Work out how long you've been alive ...

in centuries   in decades   in years

in months   in weeks

in days   in hours

in minutes   in seconds ... and counting!

 At the same time you can check out these Things You Wish You'd Invented:
2: Mobile Phone • 7: Time Zones • 10: Time Machine
31: Compass • 33: Battery • 34: Teleporter • 88: Computer

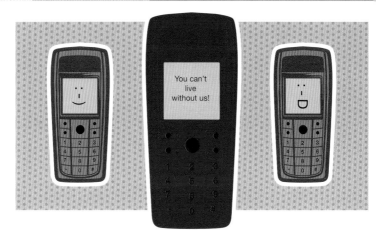

Mobile Phone

It's hard to imagine how people managed to run their lives before mobile phones
It's good to know you can get hold of your family whenever you need them,
although sometimes you might wish it wasn't so easy for them to get hold of you

C U L8r

You might have seen clunky 1980s mobile phones the size and weight of a
house brick. But did you know mobiles have been around since 1947?

- The first mobile phone system was introduced in Saint Louis in 1946 by
  US telecom companies AT&T and Southwestern Bell. This radio-telephone
  system operated in cars, and a similar one for use on the road between
  Boston and New York was introduced a year later. Both systems used a
  single transmitter and both found that there was a lot of interference.
- In 1947 Bell Laboratories came up with the idea for a cellular system –
  instead of using one large transmitter, each small area had its own low-
  powered one. This solved the interference problem.
- A cellular mobile phone network wasn't up and running for another
  thirty years. In the USA this delay was caused by strict regulation on radio
  frequencies set by the government. In 1978, Chicago had the world's first.
- Europe's first cellular mobile phones were introduced in Sweden, Finland,
  Denmark and Norway in 1981. Britain followed in 1985. At first it was
  easy to eavesdrop on other people's calls, and criminals were able to
  make calls using genuine customers' accounts. Secure networks have
  been around since the early 1990s.

Alexander Graham Bell, the inventor of the telephone in 1876, also invented an early
metal-detecting device. The story goes that when US President Garfield was shot in
1881, Bell used his metal detector to search for the bullet.

Mobile Phone **Form**

Once you have put this **Invention** to good use,
stick your Achieved Star here and fill in the form

Achieved

--- **TXT CHMPN** ---

How skilled are you with your mobile phone? Have a go at the
three challenges below. You'll find the answers at the back of the book.

--- **FASTEST FINGERS FIRST** ---

Short Messaging Service (SMS) competitions are held to find the fastest text messager on the planet. The current world record holder is Ang Chuang Yang from Singapore. He typed 160 characters in 41.52 seconds.

How fast do you think you are? See how fast you can type the message that the Guinness Book of Records officials asked him to type:

The razor-toothed piranhas of the genera Serrasalmus and Pygocentrus are the most ferocious freshwater fish in the world. In reality they seldom attack a human.

CURRENT RECORD: `4 1` . `5 2` seconds

YOUR BEST ATTEMPT: `[ ][ ]` . `[ ][ ]` seconds

If you can beat Ang Chuang Yang's time, phone the Guinness Book of Records up, quick!

--- **PHONE FRUSTRATION** ---

Some mobile phone ringtones are so annoying that you want to throw the phone as far away as possible. Well, you won't be surprised to hear that mobile phone throwing competitions have been held all over the world since 2000, when the first phone throwing contest was held in Finland.

The current world record for the furthest a mobile phone has been thrown is 94.97 m for a man and 53.52 m for a woman.

--- **TXT TST** ---

What do the following abbreviations mean?

KOTL	
LOL	
SOHF	
EOD	
FYEO	
GAL	
KISS	
PTB	
2L8	
T+	

--- **EMOTICONS** ---

What do the following represent?

----<--{@	
d-_-b	
~~>_<~~~	

At the same time you can check out these Things You Wish You'd Invented:
1: Time • 6: Photography • 13: Satellite • 23: Plastic • 33: Battery • 46: Music
52: Language • 56: World Wide Web • 71: Numbers • 75: Teenagers • 101: Room 101

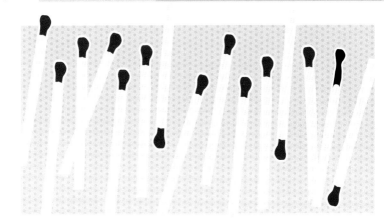

Matches

Considering how many years fire has been around, the invention of the match was a long time coming. Before matches there were various methods for lighting a fire, all of them painfully slow. The best one was a tinder box, which used steel, flint and tinder – material that would easily catch fire, such as charred cloth or flakes of wood. The tinder had to be very dry for it to work well, so it often didn't. People were desperate for something faster and more effective.

Let There Be Light

- Sticks of wood impregnated with sulphur were used in China in the sixth century. In 1680 Robert Boyle developed the same thing in England. Boyle's matches had to be handled very carefully or they caught light unexpectedly.
- K. Chancel invented a match that used sulphur, asbestos and sulphuric acid, among other things. As you can imagine, this was quite dangerous too.
- In 1826 John Walker invented a match that worked by friction. The mixture of chemicals he used on the head of the match burst into flames at low temperatures – striking it against a rough surface was enough to light one. Unfortunately this made them dangerous. And they smelled terrible, too.
- In 1845 Swedish inventor J. Lundstrom made striking a match a lot safer. His idea was to put some of the chemicals on the match head and some on the striking surface – unless the two came into contact, they wouldn't catch fire. They were known as safety matches.

Phosphorus was used in making matches until the early 20th century. It could be deadly to factory workers, who might develop 'phossy jaw', a terrible condition that made the jawbone glow in the dark and could eventually kill the sufferer.

Matches **Form**

Once you have put this **Invention** to good use,
stick your Achieved Star here and fill in the form

Achieved

----------HAVE YOU MET YOUR MATCH?----------

Can you solve the following puzzles without overlapping any matches or leaving
any loose ends? Solve the puzzles then baffle others with them to earn your star.

Puzzle 1
Can you make four complete squares
by moving only three matches?

Puzzle 2
Can you make two squares
by removing two matches?

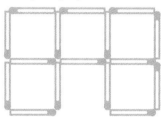

Puzzle 3
Can you make the fish face the other
way by moving only three matches?

Puzzle 4
Can you make three complete
squares by moving only three matches?

Puzzle 5
Can you make four complete
triangles by moving only two matches?

Give up? OK, then,
you'll find the answers
at the back of the book ...

 At the same time you can check out these **Things You Wish You'd Invented**:
12: Dynamite • 65: Gunpowder • 70: Fireworks

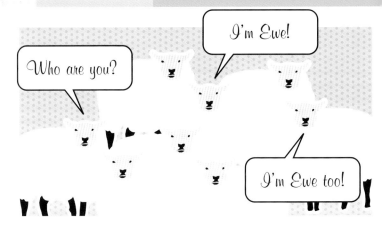

Cloning

Is it only a matter of time before there are thousands of copies of you running about confusing everybody?

Copy Cat

A clone is an exact copy of another plant or animal: the genes in both organisms are identical. Dolly, the first sheep to make history, was born on 5 July 1996 at the Roslin Institute in Scotland. Animals had been cloned before using cells from embryos, but Dolly was cloned from a cell in an adult animal. Scientists at Roslin had taken an egg from a sheep, all the genetic material, and replaced it with a cell from Dolly's mum.

This sounds like an awful lot of trouble to go to just for a sheep – after all, there are millions of the creatures and they all look exactly the same anyway. The point of cloning isn't to make identical sheep, though, it's to make it easier to produce animals or plants with particular characteristics. If animals were bred in the usual way, this would take a lot longer than with cloning. For example, sheep have been genetically engineered through cloning to produce human insulin. In the future, animals could be produced to provide human spare parts, like hearts, kidneys and livers. Another benefit of cloning might be to breed endangered animals: an Asian ox called a gaur was born to an ordinary cow in Iowa, USA, as a result of cloning.

Not surprisingly, cloning is the subject of heated debate.

Goodbye, Dolly! Dolly died at the age of six, half the usual lifespan of a sheep, suffering from cancer and arthritis. It's not known if her early death was due to the fact she was cloned. Dolly was named after country-and-western singer Dolly Parton.

Cloning **Form**

Once you have put this **Invention** to good use,
stick your Achieved Star here and fill in the form

Achieved

SEEING DOUBLE

So you think you haven't been cloned – but since there are six billion people in the world,
it would be impossible to know for sure. Not only could your double be out there
somewhere, but identity theft means they might steal your name too. Who are these people?
Use the internet to identify the impostors.

SAME-NAME IMPOSTORS

Firstly, if you live in the UK, type your name into
yourenotme.com. How many people did you
find with the same name as you? (If you're in the
USA, visit howmanyofme.com.)

[0 0 0 0 0] people in the UK/USA*
have the same name as me
*delete as appropriate

Secondly, type your name into a search engine
to see how many of your same-name impostors
have details about themselves on the internet.

How many same-name
impostors did you uncover? [0 0 0]

From your research, did you find you
have anything else in common with them? [Y/N]
If yes, list some similarities below.

[ ]

Tick the box if you found any same-name
impostors that ...

Are famous	Live nearby	Have a job you'd love	Are in prison	Have invented something	Are dead
[ ]	[ ]	[ ]	[ ]	[ ]	[ ]

Have you met any of your
same-name impostors? [Y/N]

If yes, what were they like?

☆ ☆ ☆ ☆ ☆
Nothing   A little bit   50/50   A lot   This is
like me   like me   like me uncanny

DOPPELGÄNGERS

If you're a twin, finding your *doppelgänger*
(German word meaning look-a-like or evil twin)
is going to be very easy. If not, then your
doppelganger may be extremely difficult to
find. If you haven't found your doppelgänger
already, you may be able to find one by using
the website findmydouble.com.

Have you ever seen your double? [Y/N]

If yes, where did you see them?

I have a twin brother/sister	In the street	In a photograph	At school	Other
[ ]	[ ]	[ ]	[ ]	[ ]

If other, where did you see your doppelgänger?

[ ]

Have you ever been mistaken for
someone else or been told 'you look
exactly like my friend ...'? [Y/N]

Have you met any of your
doppelgangers? [Y/N]

If yes, how much did they look like you?

☆ ☆ ☆ ☆ ☆
Nothing   A little bit   50/50   A lot   This is
like me   like me   like me uncanny

At the same time you can check out these **Things You Wish You'd Invented:**
30: Magic • 49: Homework Machine • 55: Duplication Machine • 98: Terraforming

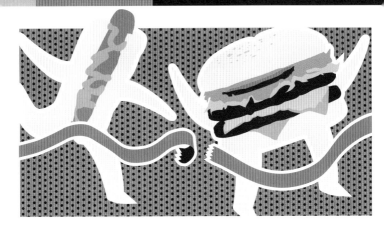

Fast Food

There's plenty of food that's quick – in fact, instant: bananas, for example. But most people think of fast food as pre-prepared meals that are heated up as soon as you order them and whisked to you in seconds.

Speedy Snacker

Fast food has been around for a long time, but it took the last 100 years or so to make it really unhealthy. The first fast food was sold from street stalls in the earliest cities in the world. The ancient Romans had stalls selling hot and cold snacks such as stews, pies and sausages. The delicious Indian fast food that's still sold in the street has followed the same recipes for centuries.

Modern fast food began when, in 1902, ready-made meals were sold in coin-operated machines in a cafe called Horn & Hardart's Automat in Philadelphia, and then ten years later in New York. It doesn't sound very appetising, but the food became popular in the 1920s and 30s during the Great Depression. People started to buy cheap ready-made take-away food instead of always cooking themselves or eating out.

The biggest fast-food restaurant chain ever is McDonald's. It started in 1948 as a restaurant run by two brothers, selling a limited menu very cheaply and quickly. They shifted so many burgers, fries and milkshakes that Ray Kroc, a milkshake-mixer salesman, decided to buy the business. Kroc's clever marketing made McDonald's the huge chain of restaurants we know today.

The healthy alternative ... In many parts of the world you can buy insect snacks, including grasshoppers, locusts, crickets and beetles. In parts of Africa, termites are roasted and eaten by the handful. They're much more nutritious than a bag of chips.

Fast Food Form

Once you have put this **Invention** to good use,
stick your Achieved Star here and fill in the form

Achieved

——— DO YOU WANT HEALTHY FRIES WITH THAT? ———

Fast food doesn't have to be an unhealthy affair, in fact more often than not the healthy version
tastes far nicer than the unhealthy one! Have a look at the fast-food recipes below and make your
own healthy smoothie, burger and fries.

——— BURGER ———

MAIN INGREDIENTS

an onion, a courgette,
an egg, 450 g minced lamb,
1 tbsp tomato puree,
fresh mint, fresh coriander,
50 g fresh breadcrumbs

ACCOMPANIMENTS

pitta bread, low-fat yoghurt,
lemon juice, fresh mint, salad

——— WHAT TO DO ———

1. Chop the onion, courgette
and fresh herbs finely and beat
the egg. Then mix and bind all
the main ingredients together
with clean hands. Make sure
you have a big enough bowl
so that you don't lose the
mixture over the side!

2. Divide your mixture into four
separate but same-size balls.

3. Take each ball in turn and
pat it into the shape of a
burger between the palms
of your hands.

4. Barbecue or grill them at
a high heat for approximately
ten minutes. Then turn them
over and grill the other side.
Keep a close watch on them
to make sure they don't burn.

5. In a separate dish mix
the low-fat yoghurt, some
chopped mint and lemon juice.
When the burgers are ready,
serve in a pitta with salad
and your minty sauce.

——— CHIPS ———

WHAT YOU NEED

Sweet potatoes, olive oil,
Worcestershire sauce,
salt, pepper

——— WHAT TO DO ———

1. Peel the potatoes and cut
out any nasty bits you find.

2. Slice the potatoes into
chunky chip shapes
(the bigger the chips are
the less fat they hold).

3. Place your chunky chips
on a baking tray and brush
them with the oil and, if you
like, Worcestershire sauce.
Season with salt and pepper
and place in a preheated oven
(200°C/400°F/gas mark 6).

4. Bake the chips until they
look a bit crispy. Test them
with a fork to see if they are
cooked through. You could do
a taste test too, but be careful
– the chips will be very hot.

5. Serve your chips with
your healthy burger or on
their own with the usual
accompaniments, such as
vinegar and ketchup. Or
you could try dipping the
chips in hummus instead
of tomato sauce to make
them even healthier.

——— SMOOTHIE ———

From the list of ingredients
below, pick at least three
different items to make an
experimental smoothie.

Bananas, apple, strawberries,
raspberries, cherries, mango,
melon, peach, pineapple, low
fat yoghurt, vanilla extract,
maple syrup, honey, mint,
semi-skimmed milk, tofu,
orange juice, coconut, ginger,
nutmeg, cinnamon.

——— WHAT TO DO ———

1. Place all your chosen
ingredients in a blender
and blend for 30 seconds
on high speed. Add ice to
the mix and keep blending
until the mixture is smooth.

Which ingredients did
you choose? Ingredient 1

Ingredient 2

Ingredient 3

Ingredient 4

How did it taste?

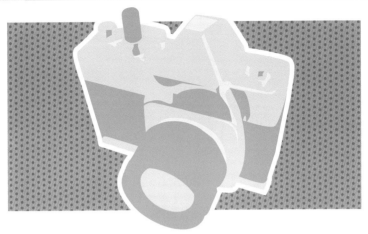

Photography

Most people keep photos as a reminder of special people and moments. Unfortunately, photos can also remind us of all our bad hair days and fashion blunders ...

Say Cheese!

People have known how to project images using a pinhole camera for thousands of years – they were using them in China 2,500 years ago. But no one managed to get a permanent image until the 1800s.

- The first ever photograph was taken in 1826 by French inventor Nicéphore Niépce. He used a pinhole camera to project the view from his window on to a photo-sensitive silver-compound-coated metal plate. It took eight hours of bright sunlight to make the image permanent!
- Louis Daguerre teamed up with Niépce and improved and developed the process. Daguerre took the first photo of a person in 1838. Even though it's a street scene, there's only one visible person in the photo, a man having his boots polished; anyone or anything that didn't stay still for at least ten minutes wouldn't show up. (That's why Victorians look so stiff in photos.)
- Around the same time, William Talbot was busy inventing a method of taking a negative print, from which any number of photographs could be made. The oldest surviving negative dates from 1835: a rather unexciting image of one of the windows in Talbot's home. Daguerre's and Talbot's inventions were the two basic processes used for photography.

 Snappy shots: At the end of the 19th century George Eastman invented the first camera that used a roll of film: the Kodak Number 1 camera. His invention meant that you didn't have to be an expert to take a photo and led to the technology used by film cameras today.

Photography **Form**

Once you have put this **Invention** to good use,
stick your Achieved Star here and fill in the form

Achieved

ONE FOR THE ALBUM

Place your favourite photographs from those you've taken in the spaces indicated below. Or you could start from scratch and make a project out of photographing all the subjects as beautifully as possible to earn your star.

Place your favourite self-portrait photograph here

Place your favourite urban photograph here

Place your favourite photograph of a funny moment here

Place your favourite photograph from an aeroplane here

Place your favourite photograph of a landscape here

Place your favourite occasion photograph here

Place your favourite animal photograph here

Place your favourite action photograph here

Place your favourite random photograph here

 At the same time you can check out these Things You Wish You'd Invented:
2: Mobile Phone • 11: Fingerprinting • 30: Magic • 37: Fashion
50: Printing • 56: World Wide Web • 59: Glass • 72: X-ray • 88: Computer

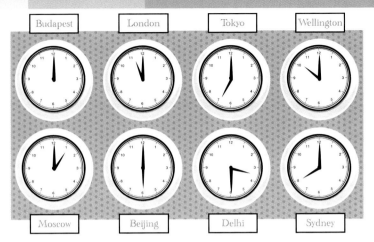

Budapest   London   Tokyo   Wellington

Moscow   Beijing   Delhi   Sydney

Time Zones

It would be very confusing if the clock said midday in one place and the sun was high in the sky, but in another place at midday the sky was pitch-black and full of stars. Thank goodness someone had the bright idea of time zones.

Universal Time

Depending where you are on the planet, it might be the middle of the day or the middle of the night, because the Earth is orbiting the Sun. Of course, before time zones clocks weren't set at the same time for everyone and no one ate their lunch at 3 a.m. or had breakfast at bedtime. People used the Sun as their guide and the time was set locally – when the Sun was overhead, it was midday. As new ways to travel and communicate were invented, knowing the exact time in different parts of the world became more and more important, and a standard time was needed.

Sir Sandford Fleming first proposed time zones for the whole world in 1876. In 1884 an international conference at the Royal Observatory in Greenwich, London, adopted the time zones we know today. Planet Earth rotates on its axis 15 degrees every hour, so the world is divided into 24 15-degree sections, with the clocks in each section set an hour apart (at least, that's how it works for most of the world). The zones are all measured from Greenwich, which the 1884 conference decided was the Prime Meridian. The time at Greenwich is known as Greenwich Mean Time or, more grandly, Universal Time.

Time out: The Pacific country of Kiribati used to have two different time zones. The eastern half of the country was a whole day and two hours behind the western half! In 1995 the time zone was changed so that Kiribati clocks all told the same time.

Time Zones **Form**

Once you have put this **Invention** to good use,
stick your Achieved Star here and fill in the form

Achieved

TIME ZONES

IN THE ZONE

The diagram above gives an approximate idea of the various time zones around the world.

Time zones are incredibly intricate and would be impossible to detail accurately here. For example, Iceland is actually in the same time zone as England even though it is thousands of miles away.

Using this standardised map, can you work out how many time zones you've been in?

If and when you've visited a time zone, colour it in. Flying through a time zone doesn't count. Only standing or sailing in a time zone earns you the right to colour it in. Next time you go on holiday, try to persuade your parents to travel to a time zone that you've never visited before.

At the same time you can check out these **Things You Wish You'd Invented:**
1: Time • 10: Time Machine • 34: Teleporter • 56: World Wide Web
60: Inter-Stellar Travel • 87: Passport • 90: Maps

Nuclear Weapons

When the first atomic bomb was dropped in 1945 it changed the world for ever. Many people wish it had never been invented at all.

Splitting the Atom

The idea for a weapon made from atomic energy had been around since Albert Einstein came up with his equation $E = MC^2$ (which means there's an awful lot of energy in absolutely everything – inside atoms). During the Second World War, when many countries were carrying out bombing campaigns on one another, the race was on to find a bomb that used the power of atoms.

Getting at the energy inside atoms isn't easy: for that you have to split them (this is called nuclear fission). Atoms are the tiny units of matter everything is made of and they are a million times smaller than the width of one of the hairs on your head. So you can imagine how tricky it is to split one. The top secret Manhattan Project in America gathered together some of the brainiest scientists in the world to try and manage it. Eventually, they succeeded. In 1945 two fission (or atomic) bombs were dropped on the Japanese cities of Nagasaki and Hiroshima, killing more than 200,000 people. Some people argue that the bombs *saved* lives because they ended the Second World War.

Nuclear fusion was developed soon after. This new way of releasing atomic power produces weapons hundreds of times more powerful than atomic bombs. They've never been used in warfare. Let's hope they never will be.

 Peace lanterns: On the anniversary of the 1945 bombing, 6 August, people float lanterns on the rivers of Hiroshima. The lanterns contain the names of people who died in the nuclear attacks and other conflicts, or messages about peace.

Nuclear Weapons **Form**

Once you have put this **Invention** to good use,
stick your Achieved Star here and fill in the form

Achieved

NEW CLEAR ANSWERS

Test your knowledge with the quiz below. Once you've completed it,
memorise the correct facts, then impress your friends to earn your star.

1. Which year saw the first ever use of a
   nuclear weapon in military action?

   a) 1918
   b) 1945
   c) 1957
   d) 1963

2. How many people are estimated to
   have died from the nuclear bomb
   dropped on Hiroshima and its
   after-effects?

   a) 1,400
   b) 14,000
   c) 140,000
   d) 1,400,000

3. How many nuclear weapons have
   been used in military action?

   a) 1
   b) 2
   c) 3
   d) 4

4. What does A-bomb stand for?

   a) Apocalyptic bomb
   b) Atomic bomb
   c) Acid fusion bomb
   d) Abrupt bomb

5. What type of climate is predicted if
   there were to be a nuclear war?

   a) A nuclear spring
   b) A nuclear summer
   c) A nuclear autumn
   d) A nuclear winter

6. Which is the most powerful weapon
   from the list below?

   a) A nuclear fission A-bomb
   b) A nuclear fusion H-bomb
   c) A conventional bomb
   d) They all do the same
      amount of damage

7. How does a nuclear
   fusion explosion work?

   a) By duplicating atoms
   b) By shrinking atoms to
      make the nuclei smaller
   c) By joining atoms together
      to make heavier nuclei
   d) By cooling atoms down

8. How does a nuclear
   fission explosion work?

   a) By joining atoms
   b) By splitting atoms
   c) By destroying atoms
   d) By heating atoms

9. Apart from in nuclear weapons,
   where else can you find radiation?

   a) Sun
   b) Microwave ovens
   c) X-ray machines
   d) All of the above

Answers at the
back of the book

At the same time you can check out these Things You Wish You'd Invented:
13: Satellite • 26: Submarine • 57: Concrete • 60: Inter-Stellar Travel
76: Intelligent Robots • 81: Laser • 88: Computer • 101: Room 101

Money

Before money, people got along by swapping things they had for things they needed. You can see how difficult this could become: what happens if you have a herd of sheep and need some clothes, but the tailor only wants potatoes? And how many potatoes make a pair of trousers, anyway?

The Colour of Money

Then someone, somewhere had a brainwave: money. Well, it probably didn't happen quite like that ...

- The first units of money were valuable in themselves – cowrie shells in ancient China around 1200 BC and other parts of the world, small amounts of grain in ancient Babylon, salt in the Roman Empire, and precious metals in many different places.
- The first metal coins were made in Lydia (modern-day Turkey) about 640 BC.
- Paper money is useful because it's a lot lighter than coins. It was first used in China from the 800s, when it was known as 'flying cash'! Elsewhere in the world paper money wasn't used for centuries.
- Credit cards were invented in the 1950s ... plenty of people probably wish they hadn't been.

> **Curious Cash**
>
> The following have all been used as money in different parts of the world:
>
> Pepper – Europe
>
> Stones – Pacific Islands (on Yap in Micronesia, stone money is still used)
>
> Coils of red feathers – Pacific Islands
>
> Dogs' teeth – New Guinea
>
> Bread – Iraq
>
> Iron nails – Scotland
>
> Whales' teeth – Fiji

 Money – who needs it? The Inca people of South America used gold and silver to make beautiful objects but they didn't use it, or anything else, as money. They seem to be one of the only civilisations that managed to do without it.

Money Form

Once you have put this **Invention** to good use,
stick your Achieved Star here and fill in the form

Achieved

WHO NEEDS MONEY?

Before the invention of money, to be able to get what you wanted you had to exchange items. This kind of trading can still be done today: in July 2005, Kyle MacDonald began his quest to own a house by swapping items. He started with a paper clip, and a year and fourteen swaps later (including swapping a doorknob, snow globe and a film role), he now owns a house.

STARTING ITEM Place a picture of the item you want to start trading with here. When you trade this item, place a picture ...	**FIRST SWAP** ... here of the next item. When you trade this item, place a picture ...	**SECOND SWAP** ... here of the next item. When you trade this item, place a picture ...	**THIRD SWAP** ... here of the next item. When you trade this item, place a picture ...
FOURTH SWAP ... here of the next item. When you trade this item, place a picture ...	**FIFTH SWAP** ... here of the next item. When you trade this item, place a picture ...	**SIXTH SWAP** ... here of the next item. When you trade this item, place a picture ...	**SEVENTH SWAP** ... here of the next item. When you trade this item, place a picture ...
EIGHTH SWAP ... here of the next item. When you trade this item, place a picture ...	**NINTH SWAP** ... here of the next item. When you trade this item, place a picture ...	**TENTH SWAP** ... here of the next item. When you trade this item, place a picture ...	**ELEVENTH SWAP** ... here of the next item. When you trade this item, place a picture ...
TWELFTH SWAP ... here of the next item. When you trade this item, place a picture ...	**THIRTEENTH SWAP** ... here of the next item. When you trade this item, place a picture ...	**FOURTEENTH SWAP** ... here of the next item. When you trade this item, place a picture of your final trade ...	**END ITEM** ... here. Did you end up with something as good as a house?

At the same time you can check out these **Things You Wish You'd Invented:**
10: Time Machine • 11: Fingerprinting • 12: Dynamite
14: Playing Cards • 22: Prison • 55: Duplication Machine • 62: Bling

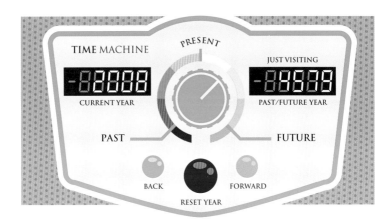

Time Machine

Do you wish you could fast-forward a few years and find out whether you will become rich and famous? Or travel to the distant future and marvel at all the new inventions? If so, get to work inventing a time machine.

Futurama

H. G. Wells's 1895 novel *The Time Machine* fired people's imaginations about time travel. Then, in 1905, Einstein's Theory of Special Relativity made it seem possible. His theory says that time isn't constant but slows down the faster you go – and the theory has since been proved (admittedly, you have to be going very fast indeed). Some scientists have theorised that, if it were possible to travel at the speed of light, we could go backwards in time. (Einstein decided it meant that travel at the speed of light is impossible.)

Other time-travel theories involve wormholes in spacetime, black holes and other mysterious bits of physics. But you probably won't be surprised that no one has actually managed to build a time machine ... yet.

There's a big problem that any time machine would have to overcome: if you travel backwards in time, you can alter the future. And if you travel to the future and then come back to the present, that can alter the future too. But if you can get round this basic paradox, come up with some extremely sophisticated technology, and understand an awful lot of complicated physics, perhaps you can become the inventor of the first time machine.

A Time Traveller Convention was held at Massachusetts Institute of Technology in 2005 in the hope of attracting visitors from the future – 300 people attended, none of them was from the future, but the event continues to be advertised so that future time travellers might go ...

Time Machine **Form**

Once you have put this **Invention** to good use,
stick your Achieved Star here and fill in the form

Achieved

PLENTY OF TIME

If you had a time machine, where would you go and what period of
time would you investigate? Make a list of the years you'd like to visit.

PAST IT

Dinosaurs! Romans! Pirates! Ancient Egypt!
Henry VIII! Shakespeare! Where in history
would you visit and why?

Name the top three places/people/time periods
you'd visit from the past in your time machine

IN THE FUTURE

In the future will cars fly? Will robots be our ally
or will they be our enemy? Will we have left
Earth behind and colonised Mars?

Name three things you'd like to see in the
future with your time machine

BLEND IN

To be a successful time traveller you'll need to master blending in with the locals. When travelling to the
past, wearing your own clothes, talking about modern life or making predictions about things that you
know will happen in the future will probably land you in trouble. You might be burnt at the stake for being
a witch. Make sure you get all the up-to-date injections from your doctor before you go, as you don't
want to travel to the past and contract the bubonic plague or some extinct disease and bring it back to
the present. On the other hand, you don't want to travel to the past with a common cold either and then
kill off half of the population of the world. If that happened, you might wipe out your own family tree and
then you'd disappear, as if you were never born in the first place!

PAST IT

If you could travel to the past and change one
thing in history, what would it be?

IN THE FUTURE

If you could visit yourself in 20 years' time,
what would you hope to find?

At the same time you can check out these **Things You Wish You'd Invented:**
1: Time • 7: Time Zones • 9: Money • 30: Magic • 34: Teleporter
60: Inter-Stellar Travel • 76: Intelligent Robots • 96: Know-It-All Hat

Fingerprinting

No two people have the same pattern of marks on the tips of their fingers ... not even identical twins. This discovery revolutionised crime detection.

Caught Red-Handed

- A scientist called Nehemiah Grew was the first person to study people's fingertip patterns and he published a book of drawings of them in 1684. It was nearly 200 years before anyone realised how useful this might be.
- In the 1860s an English civil servant called William Herschel became interested in fingertip patterns and discovered that people's fingerprints remain the same for life. His findings were published in a scientific journal.
- Francis Galton, an explorer and anthropologist, devised a system of grouping fingerprints by the different characteristics in their patterns.
- Police officer Edward Henry used Galton's system to create a comprehensive classification of fingerprints, which was published in 1900.
- The following year the first United Kingdom Fingerprint Bureau was set up in Scotland Yard, the UK police headquarters.
- Fingerprints were taken and collected together so that prints found at crime scenes could be used to link suspects with the scene of the crime.
- In 1905 fingerprinting was used for the first time to convict criminals in a murder case, in a robbery and double murder in London.

Since then, fingerprints have been used countless times to prosecute criminals all over the world.

Wrapped around your finger: Francis Galton thought that fingerprints might be a sign of a person's intelligence. He designed his system of classifying prints for measuring intelligence – but instead it was used for catching criminals.

Fingerprinting Form

Once you have put this **Invention** to good use,
stick your Achieved Star here and fill in the form

Achieved

--- **YOU'RE NICKED!** ---

Before you attempt this form, photocopy this page several times, then leave your fingerprints below.
On the copies, take prints of the rest of your family and friends and file them away in a crime
folder. When you get blamed for a crime you didn't commit, dust for prints and find the real culprit.

First name

Height   Weight

$\boxed{0} . \boxed{0\ 0}$ m / $\boxed{0\ 0\ 0}$ kg

Surname

Distinguishing features

Date of birth

d d m m y y y y

Affix photo here

1. RIGHT THUMB	2. RIGHT INDEX	3. RIGHT MIDDLE	4. RIGHT RING	5. RIGHT LITTLE
1. LEFT THUMB	2. LEFT INDEX	3. LEFT MIDDLE	4. LEFT RING	5. LEFT LITTLE

--- **DUSTING FOR PRINTS** ---

Successfully solved cases:

When dusting for prints, use
cocoa powder (the powder
doesn't have to be white as long
as it is fine) and a fine brush.
Dusting works best on glass or
smooth surfaces. Finally, match
the prints up to the correct culprit
and clear your name!

At the same time you can check out these Things You Wish You'd Invented:
6: Photography • 9: Money • 12: Dynamite • 22: Prison
28: Lie Detector • 59: Glass • 65: Gunpowder • 85: Mirror

Dynamite

Without dynamite we wouldn't be able to blow things up in a spectacular but relatively safe way. And without dynamite, we wouldn't have the Nobel Prize.

Tick, Tick, Tick ... Boom!

Large explosions are pretty dangerous by nature. But they're also very useful in industries like quarrying and mining. Before dynamite was invented, explosives such as gunpowder were used – the problem was their tendency to explode when people were least expecting it. Swedish inventor Alfred Nobel discovered that nitroglycerine, another very dangerous explosive, could be mixed with a special absorbent sand to make it safe enough to use. He called his invention 'Nobel's Safety Powder' before realising that 'dynamite', from the Greek word for power, sounded a lot more catchy. Nobel went on to invent another explosive, gelignite, which was even more powerful than dynamite.

Dynamite made blowing up quarries a much safer affair, but it could also be used in warfare. In 1888 a French newspaper made a mistake and published an obituary for Alfred Nobel even though he wasn't dead. The article said 'the merchant of death is dead' (except in French) and condemned Nobel for an invention that killed people more efficiently than ever before. Alfred read the article and changed his will: he used his fortune to set up the Nobel Prizes, which are still awarded every year for outstanding achievements in physics, chemistry, medicine, literature, and for work in peace.

 A dangerous business: The Nobel family owned a factory where, not surprisingly, there were several explosions. The worst of them happened in 1864 when several workers, including Alfred's brother Emil, were killed.

Dynamite **Form**

Once you have put this **Invention** to good use,
stick your Achieved Star here and fill in the form

Achieved

KA-BOOM!!!!!

In the Wild West dynamite was hijacked by criminals and used for bank heists, safe-cracking and train robberies. Can you match the famous outlaws and lawmen below to their real names and other facts about them? Answers at the back of the book.

WANTED: DEAD OR ALIVE

OUTLAW

Ned Kelly	Billy the Kid	Butch Cassidy	Wild Bill
Clyde	Buffalo Bill	Jesse James	Wyatt Earp

REAL NAME

James Butler Hickok	William L. Brooks	Jesse Woodson James	Robert LeRoy Parker
Henry McCarty	Wyatt Berry Stapp Earp	Clyde Barrow	Edward Kelly

OCCUPATION

Train and bank robber	Murderer, robber and kidnapper	Lawman turned outlaw	Lawman and saloon keeper
Bank robber	Lawman	Bushranger	Feuding gunfighter

ACCOMPLICE

Doc Holliday	William 'Buffalo Bill' Cody	None	Bonnie Parker
Sundance Kid	Jesse Evans	Cole Younger	Dan Kelly

KILLER FACTS

Formed a gang known as the 'Wild Bunch'	Became marshal of Newton, Kansas	Tried to escape in a suit of armour and failed	Fought in the American Civil War
Killed cowboy Davis Tutt in a quick-draw shootout	Involved in the gunfight at the O.K. Corral	Masterminded a jailbreak at the Texas Department of Corrections	Killed 21 men, one for each year of his life

HOW DID THEY DIE?

Died of natural causes	Ambushed	Uncertain	Hanged
Shot by Sheriff Pat Garrett	Killed by a lynch mob before his trial	Shot by a gang member while dusting	Shot during a poker game

---

At the same time you can check out these **Things You Wish You'd Invented:**
3: Matches • 9: Money • 11: Fingerprinting
20: Thermometer • 22: Prison • 65: Gunpowder • 70: Fireworks

Satellite

Did you know that you're on a satellite right now? No, not the armchair – planet Earth.

Into Orbit

A satellite is an object that is in orbit around another one – the Earth orbits the Sun and the Moon orbits the Earth because of the force of gravity. The little bits of rock and ice in the asteroid belt are all satellites. But there are artificial satellites too, far above your head, in orbit around the Earth.

In 1957 the USSR launched Sputnik 1, the first artificial satellite. Sputnik weighed just 83 kg, took about 98 minutes to orbit the Earth, and was used to conduct experiments on the atmosphere. After the Second World War, the USA and the USSR (now split into Russia and other countries) were bitter rivals. The Americans must have been very annoyed indeed that their rivals had done something they hadn't, and they were aware that there were all sorts of uses for satellites, including spying. The following year, the USA launched its first satellite, Explorer 1 – the 'Space Race' was on.

Now there are tens of thousands of artificial satellites in orbit above the Earth. There are satellites for communication, navigation, monitoring the weather, observing the Earth and scientific research. Since we use them for making phone calls, watching TV, finding our way and forecasting the weather, life wouldn't be the same without them.

A month after Sputnik 1, the USSR sent the first living creature into space on Sputnik 2 – a dog called Laika. Since then, lots more living things have been sent into space, including humans (Soviet Yuri Gagarin was the first), spiders, bees, frogs and jellyfish.

Satellite **Form**

Once you have put this **Invention** to good use,
stick your Achieved Star here and fill in the form

Achieved

SATELLITE SPOTTING

Earth has over 8,000 artificial satellites and one natural one. Have you spotted a satellite before? If not, here are some tips on what to look for and how to find them. Tick the boxes below once you've spotted each one. Earn your star when you've spotted at least three of the five.

The Moon
This is Earth's only natural satellite and the easiest to spot – just look up in the sky on a reasonably clear night and there it is. But did you know that the Moon is slowly moving away from us? Each year it moves 3.8 cm further away from the Earth. At present the Moon is 400 times smaller than the Sun, and coincidentally it's 400 times closer to Earth, which means we are able to see very impressive solar eclipses. As the Moon moves away, total eclipses will become a thing of the past. For a list of the next solar eclipses and where to view them, visit this link: http://sunearth.gsfc.nasa.gov/eclipse/eclipse.html

The International Space Station (ISS)
The first section of the ISS was launched in November 1998 and the very first crew joined the station two years later in November 2000. It has been inhabited ever since. On the 35th anniversary of Alan Shepard's golf swing on the Moon, Mikhail Tyurin, a Russian cosmonaut aboard the ISS, hit a golf ball, making it into the record books for the furthest golf ball drive. Track the ISS (but unfortunately not the golf ball) by visiting this link: http://spaceflight.nasa.gov/realdata/tracking

The Space Shuttle
If you see a space shuttle in the night sky, you're looking at one of three shuttles that are still in service (*Atlantis*, *Discovery* or *Endeavour*). The first manned shuttle mission began with *Columbia*, April 1981. Since then the shuttle fleet has flown over one hundred missions and is due to fly many more before it retires in 2010. So visit the link and see the shuttle in orbit before it is taken out of service for ever: http://spaceflight1.nasa.gov/realdata/tracking/

Spy Satellites & Space Junk
You're not supposed to know about these satellites, so here's a tip: the best way to spot a spy satellite is by its orbit. Spy satellites travel north to south! To track the Cosmos 1222 spy satellite, go to www.heavens-above.com/selectsat.asp?lat=0&lng=0&loc= Unspecified&alt=0&tz=CET and in the satellite name box, type Cosmos 1222 and click submit – when you spot the satellite, keep an eye out for space junk. It is followed by the spent rocket that launched it!

Hubble Space Telescope (HST)
The Hubble Space Telescope is an incredible camera. It has taken some of the most amazing pictures it has ever likely to see. Over the last eighteen years it has photographed stars being born, stars dying and it's even been able to look back in time by photographing galaxies millions of miles away. To track the Hubble Space Telescope and many other satellites, visit this link: http://science.nasa.gov/realtime/jtrack/Spacecraft.html

For more information, visit the following sites: www.nasa.gov & www.heavens-above.com

At the same time you can check out these **Things You Wish You'd Invented:**
2: Mobile Phone • 31: Compass • 47: Radar • 56: World Wide Web • 60: Inter-Stellar Travel • 61: Microscope and Telescope • 88: Computer • 96: Know-It-All Hat

Playing Cards

Ever played Bridge, Gin Rummy, Cribbage, Whist, Poker ... Snap? Or maybe you've built a house of cards or performed card tricks? They'd all be impossible without this simple but brilliantly versatile invention.

Stacking the Deck

No one knows where playing cards were first invented: maybe in India, China or Egypt. Some people argue that the jacks, queens and kings on playing cards are drawn as they are because of their origins in ancient Egyptian hieroglyphics, which are in the same two-dimensional style. Wherever they first appeared, the Chinese were definitely playing card games in the first part of the twelfth century. Playing cards arrived in Europe around the late 1300s, probably based on the cards played with by Islamic soldiers called Mamluks. The Mamluks' cards had 52 cards in a deck and four suits.

The four suits we know today – hearts, diamonds, spades and clubs – began in France in the late 1400s. But there were and still are lots of different suits in different parts of Europe, including polo sticks, roses, helmets, horses, parrots, bears, banners, swords and cups.

At first, cards had to be hand-painted, so only very rich people could afford them. After a while playing cards were reproduced using woodcuts, and Gutenberg's printing press, invented in 1440, made printing decks of cards easier still.

 Pack animal or loner: There are tens of thousands of card games. You can play more than a thousand of them on your own: these one-player games are known as Solitaire or Patience and include Baker's Dozen, Grandfather's Clock and Idiot's Delight.

Playing Cards **Form**

Once you have put this **Invention** to good use,
stick your Achieved Star here and fill in the form

Achieved

CARD KARMA

There are many thousands of card games out there, far too many to list below, so here is an
old favourite. It's a great card game called 'Karma', although it does go by other names. Try it.
To earn your star, win the best of five games.

HOW TO PLAY

This game is for two or three players but can be altered to include more players. The idea is to be the first person to get rid of all your cards. The loser may be given a forfeit for losing, but be careful when handing out punishments. You're not going to win all the games and your opponents will want retribution.

In this game 2's are the highest cards, followed by ace, then king, queen, jack, 10, 9, 8, 7, 6, 5, 4 and, finally, 3.

The person whose birthday it is next deals first.

1. Firstly, the dealer deals three cards, face down in a row, to each player. These cards can only be looked at in the final part of the game.

2. Then the dealer deals to each player again, this time placing three cards face up on top of the first three cards.

3. A further three cards are dealt, face down, to each player. The players pick up these cards. The remaining cards are placed face down in the centre of the table.

4. Look at your hand and the face-up cards on your three piles. You can change all the top cards on the piles for the cards in your hand if you wish. It is best to have high cards left face up on the table. You are better off having lower cards (with the exception of 2's) in your hand to start with.

6. The play starts with whoever has a 3: this card is laid in the centre of the table face up, next to the face-down pack. If more than one person has a 3, the person closest to the dealer lays their card. If there are no 3's then start with a 4 or the next lowest card.

7. Each player must play a card and then pick up a new card from the pack. Always have 3 cards in your hand unless you've had to pick up the pile of laid-down cards (see 12). You must either place the same card number that has already been played or something higher. It is always best to get rid of your lower cards first.

8. If you cannot lay a higher card or a card of the same amount, you must pick up a new card from the pack, but you cannot play this straight away; you must wait until your next go.

9. If you have duplicates of the same number card then you can put them all down at the same time. For example, if on your go you have three 8's, you can play them all, but you must make sure you pick up three new cards to replace them.

10. Continue in this way until you cannot play a higher card. For example if the card on the pile is a queen and you only have a 6, 8 and 9 then you pick up until you pick up a higher card, a 2 or a 10.

11. Special Cards. 2's can be played at any time and a 2 resets the play so the next card can be a 3 or the next lowest card. 10's can also be played at any time and all the cards underneath are removed from play and cannot be used again. The whole pile is also removed if four cards of the same suit are played in a row.

12. Cards are picked up and played until all the cards run out and no more can be picked up. Keep playing until you run out of cards in your hand, BUT if you cannot play a card from your hand from this point on, you must pick up ALL the cards that have been laid down on the pile!

13. Once you have got rid of all the cards in your hand you can play the three cards lying face up in front of you on the table. Once you have played these cards then you can play the 3 face-down cards blind, one at a time, in any order, and hope that it is a higher number. If it isn't playable you must pick up all the cards in the pile.

14. The winner is the first person to get rid of all their cards, but play is continued until there is a single loser. The loser is then issued with a forfeit to complete.

At the same time you can check out these Things You Wish You'd Invented:
2: Mobile Phone • 9: Money • 15: Tattoo • 19: Birthdays • 22: Prison • 30: Magic
50: Printing • 56: World Wide Web • 62: Bling • 71: Numbers • 88: Computer

Tattoo

It might seem a strange idea, but using a sharp object to inject dye underneath the skin has been going on for a long time, and in many far-flung corners of the world ...

Scratching the Surface

- Believe it or not, we can still see the tattoos on a 5,500-year-old man. The oldest mummy ever found, known as Otzi the Ice Man, was preserved in ice in the Alps. Otzi has no fewer than 57 tattoos on his body. X-rays have shown that Otzi had arthritis in the places covered by the tattoos, so perhaps they were used as a magic charm or remedy to cure the condition.
- There are tattoos on an ancient Egyptian mummy of a priestess called Amunet from around 4,000 years ago. Ancient Egyptian clay dolls have also been discovered with similar tattoo marks on them. No one knows what the marks signified.
- A tattooed chieftain from around 2,500 years ago was found in Siberian Russia. The body is covered in tattoos of elaborate animal designs.
- People of the South Pacific have worn tattoos for hundreds of years. The complicated designs carry meanings about the wearer's status. Our word 'tattoo' may derive from a Tahitan word 'tatau', which means 'wound'.
- Tattoos are still as popular as ever. Samuel O'Reilly invented his electric tattooing machine in 1891 and modern machines can puncture the skin 3,000 times per minute, making the ancient art of tattooing a little quicker.

 Useful tattoos: Scientists have invented a 'smart tattoo' that glows to warn diabetics when their blood sugar levels are low. At the moment, people with diabetes have to prick themselves with a needle to test their blood sugar.

Tattoo **Form**

Once you have put this **Invention** to good use,
stick your Achieved Star here and fill in the form

Achieved

——————— TEMPORARILY TATTOOED ———————

It's easy to make your own temporary tattoos if you have the use of a computer and colour printer.
You'll also need special tattoo paper that can go through the printer ... oh yes, and an eye for
brilliant designs. Below is a selection of designs to get you started. There are many types of tattoo
paper, so make sure you read the instructions properly before printing. Scan these examples into
your computer or create your own using an art program, and then print them on to tattoo paper.

At the same time you can check out these Things You Wish You'd Invented:
14: Playing Cards • 21: Guitar • 22: Prison • 37: Fashion • 50: Printing • 81: Laser

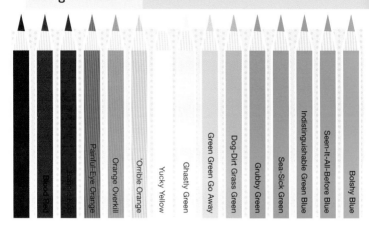

Blood Red · Fearsome Red · Painful-Eye Orange · Orange Overkill · 'Orrible Orange · Yucky Yellow · Ghastly Green · Green Green Go Away · Dog-Dirt Grass Green · Grubby Green · Sea-Sick Green · Indistinguishable Green Blue · Seen-It-All-Before Blue · Bolshy Blue

Pencils

It must have been a relief when pencils were invented – at last, an easy-to-use alternative to quills and ink. And you can rub out your mistakes, too.

Straight to the Point

The part of a pencil you write with isn't lead but graphite, a type of carbon. In 1565 a huge deposit of pure graphite was found near Borrowdale in Cumbria. People didn't know exactly what it was then, they just knew it was very useful for making marks on things – like sheep – and they called it plumbago, Latin for lead ore (that's why the graphite in pencils is often called lead). The graphite in Cumbria is the only pure kind ever found, so whoever found it is the person to thank for pencils. Soon people realised that the graphite could be used to write or draw with if it was cut into sticks and, because it's very soft, encased in a wooden holder.

Graphite was found in other parts of the world but in a much less pure form, which meant it had to be powdered and didn't make very good pencils. In 1795 Nicholas Jacques Conte, an officer in Napoleon's army, found a way of firing powdered graphite and clay in a kiln to make graphite rods that made good pencils. By varying the amounts of clay and graphite he could adjust the hardness. Now you can buy softer pencils (B, 2B, 3B, etc), harder ones (H, 2H, 3H, etc) and inbetween ones (HB). Coloured pencils weren't invented until the 1920s. They're made from colour pigments mixed with wax or oil-based binders – not graphite at all.

Here today, gone tomorrow ... Rubber erasers weren't invented until 1770, by Joseph Priestley, but before that people used bread (you should try it). In 1858 Hyman Lipman thought of attaching a small eraser to the end of a pencil.

Pencils **Form**

Once you have put this **Invention** to good use,
stick your Achieved Star here and fill in the form

Achieved

2B OR NOT 2B

Hail the mighty pencil! Use pencils to draw a picture your parents will think is good enough to put up on the wall. Add a copy of your work of art in the frame below for your records.

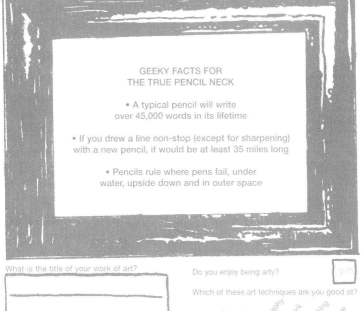

GEEKY FACTS FOR
THE TRUE PENCIL NECK

• A typical pencil will write
over 45,000 words in its lifetime

• If you drew a line non-stop (except for sharpening)
with a new pencil, it would be at least 35 miles long

• Pencils rule where pens fail, under
water, upside down and in outer space

What is the title of your work of art?

Do you enjoy being arty? [y/n]

Which of these art techniques are you good at?

How do you rate this piece?

Drawing Painting Photography Woodwork Printmaking Sculpture Doodling

☆ ☆ ☆ ☆ ☆

Awful OK Good Great Excellent

Which artist do you most admire?

How long did it take you to draw?

[0,0] days [0,0] hours [0,0] mins

At the same time you can check out these Things You Wish You'd Invented:
15: Tattoo • 25: Poetry • 29: Post-it Notes • 42: School
49: Homework Machine • 50: Printing • 52: Language • 71: Numbers

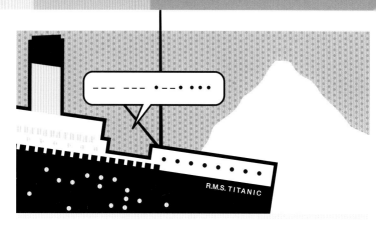

Morse Code

If ever you need to send a secret message to someone in the next room using a spanner and a pipe, you might have reason to thank Samuel Morse.

Join the Dot Dot Dots

Morse code wasn't invented to help people in dire emergencies but to send messages along a telegraph wire (this was in the 1830s – way before Instant Messaging). Samuel Morse and Alfred Vail had developed an electric device that could send signals from one machine to another, but couldn't send readable letters. Morse came up with a method of sending signals that could be received by a machine and marked on to paper as dots and dashes. Different combinations of dots and dashes correspond to letters and numbers

After a while, telegraph operators could translate the messages just by listening to the sounds made by the machines – a dot was a short click and a dash was a longer one (this is why your spanner and pipe could come in handy). Messages can also be transmitted in Morse using a light (short and long flashes for the dots and dashes), so the code was used for sending messages from one ship to another. In fact it was the international standard code at sea until 1999. Now satellite communication is used instead.

Morse code might look complicated and time-consuming, but some experiments have proved that it's quicker than texting (if you're a Morse expert). Maybe it's time for Morse code to make a comeback!

 Making a dramatic exit: When the French navy stopped using Morse code in 1997, the last message they ever transmitted was rather profound in tone: 'Calling all. This is our last cry before our eternal silence.'

Morse Code **Form**

Once you have put this **Invention** to good use,
stick your Achieved Star here and fill in the form

Achieved

— —   — — —   • — •   • • •   •   — • — •   — — —   — • • •   • —

Morse code comprises the following components:

1. a dot (or dit) – a short audio tone (represented as '•') 2. a dash (or dah) – a longer audio tone than a dot (represented as '–') 3. a very short gap between each dot and dash 4. a slightly longer gap between each letter 5. a mid-length gap between each word (represented as '/') 6. a long gap between each sentence (represented as '//') For instance, if you wanted to send the message 'Meet me at midnight', this is how it would look:

— —   •   •   —   /   — —   •   /   • —   —   /   — —   • •   — • •   — •   • •   — — •   • • • •   —
M   E   E   T   M   E   A   T   M   I   D   N   I   G   H   T

You can send your messages as a series of audible tones or by flashing a light,
using long and short flashes. Alternatively, you can write it out. Below is a
key to each letter and number in the Morse code alphabet. Make a copy for a friend and
start practising. You could even send text messages to each other in Morse code!

A • —	B — • • •	C — • — •	D — • •
E •	F • • — •	G — — •	H • • • •
I • •	J • — — —	K — • —	L • — • •
M — —	N — •	O — — —	P • — — •
Q — — • —	R • — •	S • • •	T —
U • • —	V • • • —	W • — —	X — • • —
Y — • — —	Z — — • •	1 • — — — —	2 • • — — —
3 • • • — —	4 • • • • —	5 • • • • •	6 — • • • •
7 — — • • •	8 — — — • •	9 — — — — •	0 — — — — —

SENDING   **RECEIVING**

Did you find learning/reading   How did you receive your first message?
Morse Code difficult?

How did you send your first message?

Light ☐   Sound ☐   Written ☐   What was the message?

Did the person receiving
the message understand it?

Did you make any mistakes?   Did you decipher it correctly?

At the same time you can check out these **Things You Wish You'd Invented**:
13: Satellite • 25: Poetry • 26: Submarine • 38: Sign Language
52: Language • 78: Language Decoder

Fizzy Drinks

Too many fizzy drinks can be bad for you, but the first manufactured fizzy drinks were just bubbles in water, which isn't so bad for you, just flavourless.

A Glass of Bubbly

The fizz in fizzy drinks is dissolved carbon dioxide (the same gas you breathe out). No one really invented fizzy drinks because they can occur naturally: underground volcanic action can put carbon dioxide into spring water.

The first person to copy naturally fizzy water was the English scientist Joseph Priestley. During his research into carbon dioxide, which he called 'fixed air', he discovered a way to put carbon dioxide bubbles into water by putting a bowl of water above a vat of fermenting beer. He liked the taste of his fizzy water, offered it to his friends, and began producing it in quantity in 1772. He'd developed another way of making the water fizzy, using sulphuric acid and chalk, and no longer needed huge vats of beer.

By the 19th century, fizzy mineral water had become popular, especially in the USA where the drinks were sold from 'soda fountains' in chemist shops. Manufacturers began adding flavours, such as dandelion and birch bark, which people seemed to like even though they don't sound very appetising.

Today the best known fizzy drink in the world is Coca Cola. It was intended as a medicine by its inventor, John Pemberton, at the end of the 19th century.

Joseph Priestley also invented the eraser, and discovered hydrochloric acid and various gases, including oxygen (which he called 'dephlogisticated air') and nitrous oxide, or laughing gas. He was also a leading philosopher and anti-slavery campaigner.

Fizzy Drinks **Form**

Once you have put this **Invention** to good use,
stick your Achieved Star here and fill in the form

Achieved

──── TOP OF THE POPS ────

──── MAKE A FIZZY DRINK ────

For this experiment you'll need BICARBONATE OF
SODA, ICING SUGAR and CITRIC ACID MONO-
HYDRATE POWDER. You should be able to find
the first two ingredients in a supermarket. Citric
acid powder might also be in the baking section of
the supermarket or you can try an Asian
supermarket or a chemist. YOU MUSTN'T USE
LIQUID CITRIC ACID!

──── WHAT TO DO ────

1. Take a bowl and add SIX TEASPOONS of CITRIC
ACID MONOHYDRATE POWDER to THREE
TEASPOONS of BICARBONATE OF SODA.

2. Add TWO TABLESPOONS of ICING SUGAR and
mix it all together thoroughly. You now have your fizzy
drinks mixture.

3. Put TWO TEASPOONS of your fizzy drinks mixture
in a glass and then start to fill the glass with a juice of
your choosing (e.g. apple juice). Add slowly, as it will
create a lot of froth when it comes into contact with
the powder. The bubbles that occur from the mixture
are carbon dioxide, just like the bubbles in the fizzy
drinks you normally buy. The more juice you pour into
the glass, the less fizzy the drink will become.
Experiment with different quantities and juice
flavours.

──── MAKE SHERBET ────

You can also make sherbet with the same
ingredients, but the quantities are slightly different.

1. In a clean, dry bowl mix TWO TEASPOONS of
CITRIC ACID MONOHYDRATE POWDER with ONE
TEASPOON of BICARBONATE OF SODA.

2. Now add TWO TABLESPOONS of ICING SUGAR
and mix it all together thoroughly. You now have
sherbet.

3. Now put it in your mouth – it won't taste very nice
but it'll fizz! If you want it to be sweeter, add more
ICING SUGAR. If you want it to be fizzier, add more
BICARBONATE of SODA. You might want to dip a
lolly in it to make the experience more pleasant.

──── EXPERIMENT RESULTS ────

Did you manage to make a fizzy drink?   [y/n]

Which flavour did you make?

How did it taste?

Awful   OK   Good   Great   Excellent

How long did your drink stay fizzy for?

Seconds   A minute   Just long enough to drink   Hours   I don't know, it went down the sink!

Will you make more fizzy drinks this way
in the future?   [y/n]

──── EXPERIMENT RESULTS ────

Did you manage to make fizzy sherbet?   [y/n]

How did it feel on your tongue?

How did it taste?

Awful   OK   Good   Great   Excellent

Do you think you'll be making your own
sherbet in the future?   [y/n]

 At the same time you can check out these Things You Wish You'd Invented:
5: Fast Food • 19: Birthdays • 27: Pizza • 32: Cutlery
66: Tea • 68: Refrigerator • 77: Banana Suitcase

Birthdays

Imagine if you didn't have your birthday to look forward to every year.
It would be like cancelling Christmas.

Happy Returns

People haven't always celebrated the day they were born. In prehistoric
times, people didn't have diaries to help remember their friends' and
relatives' birthdays. In fact, for much of human history, most people didn't
know the date they were born, or the date of anything else for that matter.

Ancient civilisations did celebrate birthdays – at least, important people's,
like kings' and queens'. Predictions were made based on someone's date of
birth – just like today's horoscopes. The early Jewish and Christian people
didn't celebrate birthdays because of this link with pagan fortune-telling.

Mithraism was a religion that became popular in ancient Roman times.
Followers of Mithraism decided birthdays were a good thing, and the idea of
celebrating your date of birth spread. The ancient Romans were very keen
on holidays and festivals, so this was a handy excuse for yet another one.

Today, most people celebrate the day they were born, but not everyone.
Some people are just a bit miserable about them because they don't like the
idea of getting older. Others have religious objections to birthdays, like the
early Jews and Christians did.

 'Happy Birthday to You' is not only one of the most frequently sung melodies in the world, but is one of the three songs you're most likely to hear sung in the English language. The other two are 'Auld Lang Syne' and 'For He's a Jolly Good Fellow'.

Birthdays **Form**

Once you have put this **Invention** to good use,
stick your Achieved Star here and fill in the form

Achieved

HAPPY BIRTHDAY

What makes your special day even more special? Do you know
which famous people share your birthday or what historical events happened
on it and when? Use the internet to find the answers and write them below.

What was the date and time of your birth?

d d m m y y y y   0 0 : 0 0   AM/PM

What did you weigh?   kg/lb

How 'tall' were you?   cm

Where were you born?

In hospital | At home | In a foreign country | Outside | Other

[ ] [ ] [ ] [ ] [ ]

If other, explain below

What sign of the Zodiac are you?

What is your Chinese birth sign? (e.g. Rat)

What is the best present you've ever had?

What is the worst present you've ever had?

What have you always wanted but never got?

Which famous people share your birthday?

List three historical events that coincide with your birthday

0 0 0 0   A.D / B.C

0 0 0 0   A.D / B.C

0 0 0 0   A.D / B.C

At the same time you can check out these **Things You Wish You'd Invented:**
5: Fast Food • 18: Fizzy Drinks • 30: Magic • 35: CDs and DVDs
46: Music • 51: Make-up • 62: Bling • 67: Dancing • 71: Numbers • 75: Teenagers

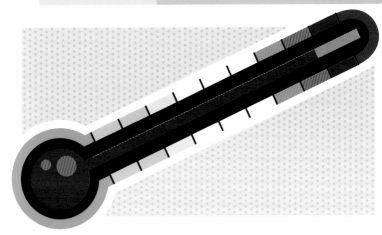

Thermometer

Before thermometers were invented no one could be very exact about temperature. As far back as the ancient Greeks, the principle that some substances, like air, expand as they get hotter and contract when they get cooler, had been observed, but it took a long time before this theory was successfully applied to the production of a device that could measure temperature.

Freezing and Boiling

- In 1592 Galileo Galilei produced a thermoscope, like a thermometer but without a scale, so it wasn't very accurate. His contemporary, an Italian doctor called Santorio, is believed to have been the first to add a numerical scale.
- In the 1680s Guillaume Amontons developed a thermometer that used mercury, which expands as it gets hotter (earlier ones used air, which isn't as effective). But Amontons' thermometer still wasn't very good.
- Gabriel Fahrenheit made a big difference to the development of the invention when he made the first successful mercury thermometer in 1714. Ten years later he came up with a temperature scale that's still used widely today.

Although Fahrenheit is still used in the USA, most people use centigrade (or Celsius) for measuring temperature. Centigrade is a *lot* more sensible: Swedish astronomer Anders Celsius came up with the scale in 1742 based on the freezing point and boiling point of water (0 degrees centigrade and 100 degrees centigrade respectively – though originally it was the other way around). Fahrenheit chose 32 degrees as the freezing point of water and 212 as the boiling point – perhaps he just liked to make things complicated.

The Kelvin temperature scale was developed in the 1880s by Lord Kelvin and is used for extremes of temperature. 0 degrees in the Kelvin scale is absolute zero – the coldest anything can get – and is equivalent to minus 273 degrees centigrade.

Thermometer **Form**

Once you have put this **Invention** to good use,
stick your Achieved Star here and fill in the form

Achieved

MAKE YOUR OWN THERMOMETER

A thermometer is a really clever piece of kit. It's hard to replicate such an
accurate device, but here is a way to create a very basic one. Build one to earn your star.

WHAT YOU NEED

water, a clear plastic bottle with lid,
a clear plastic drinking straw,
food colouring, Blu-tack

WHAT TO DO

Chill a bowl of water in the fridge overnight.

Fill a clear plastic bottle right to the top
with the tap water (1). Add a few drops of
food colouring to the water to make
the temperature change easily visible.

Cut a hole in the top of the bottle lid wide
enough for the straw to fit through (2).
Push the straw into the bottle through the
hole but don't let it touch the base of the bottle.

Take the Blu-tack and use it to seal the gaps
between the straw and the bottle top (3).

You have made a basic thermometer! Now you
need to check that it works. Let the thermometer
stand for a few hours until the water in the bottle
is at room temperature.

As the cold tap water in the bottle rises to room
temperature, so the water should rise up the
straw. Mark the new level on the straw (4).

Place your thermometer in the bowl of cold water
you kept in the fridge. Leave it to stand for 30
mins and watch as the water level falls (5).

Then place your device in the sink with hot water
and watch as the water level rises (6).

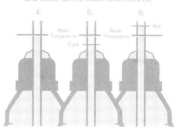

NOTE: YOU CAN REUSE THIS BOTTLE TO
MAKE A SUBMARINE (see **INVENTION** No. 26)

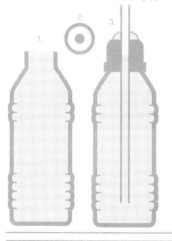

RESULTS

Did your thermometer work?

How far did the water level fall
from room temperature when
you put it in cold water?

How far did it rise when you
put it in hot water?

At the same time you can check out these Things You Wish You'd Invented:
24: Hot-Air Balloon • 26: Submarine • 27: Pizza • 43: Sliced Bread • 54: Steam Engine
68: Refrigerator • 69: Weather Machine • 73: Sunscreen • 98: Terraforming

Guitar

From the Stratocaster to the air guitar, this is one of the world's most versatile and popular instruments.

Centuries of Strumming

People have been strumming instruments similar to modern-day guitars for thousands of years.

- Sculptures from the ancient city of Susa, in modern-day Iran, show people playing instruments very like guitars. They're more than 3,500 years old.
- Ancient guitar-like instruments include the kithara and the lyre, both strummed in ancient Greece.
- The Arabic oud and the Mediterranean lute are stringed instruments like guitars, but without the guitar's distinctive curved sides and 'waist'.
- The *guitarra Latina*, which first appeared in Spain in the Middle Ages, developed into the guitar design we know today.
- Guitar design changed over the centuries. By around 1800 the instrument had the six strings of most modern instruments, and the basic design has stayed the same for about the last 150 years.
- In 1935 the electric guitar was invented by Adolph Rickenbacher and George Beauchamp (though various people had helped to develop it). The new louder sound led to a revolution in the music of popular culture.
- In 1939 Charlie Christian was the first to amaze an audience with an electric guitar solo. People have been playing air guitar ever since.

The Jimi Hendrix Experience: In May 2007 guitar players gathered in Wroclaw, Poland, to play 'Hey Joe', by the famous guitarist Jimi Hendrix. Nearly 2,000 guitarists broke the world record for the largest guitar orchestra ever.

Guitar **Form**

Once you have put this **Invention** to good use,
stick your Achieved Star here and fill in the form

Achieved

Born to Rock

If the guitar had never been invented then the air guitar would never have been born. Air guitar is quite simply the art of playing an invisible guitar. The cult of the air guitar has grown from an embarrassing dance move to a worldwide celebration of an 'art' that takes place in the form of international championships held every year to find the world's best air guitarist.

HOW TO PLAY YOUR AIR GUITAR: Remember, anyone can play air guitar – you don't need to be a guitarist and you don't need a guitar. 1. Create an awesome stage name for yourself, like Björn Túroque (pronounced Bjorn to Rock, a perennial Air Guitar World Championships participant) • 2. Turn a rock classic up to eleven on the volume dial, one that features plenty of powerchords or dirty guitar riffs, like Motörhead's 'Ace of Spades' or Iron Maiden's 'Phantom of the Opera' • 3. Leap around the room and create a winning air-guitar routine using some of the moves below • 4. Finally, look the part. Long hair is preferable, make-up is optional, a black rock T-shirt is standard and a rock attitude is essential. LET'S ROCK!

Powerslide

Take a run-up and slide across the stage on your knees while playing your 'guitar'.

Move completed ☐

Headbang

Whip your head backwards and forwards. If you have long hair, throw it across your face with the first whip. Remember to keep playing the 'guitar' throughout.

Move completed ☐

Rock Splits

Stand with your legs as far apart from each other as possible.

Move completed ☐

Rock Leap

Leap in the air while playing your 'guitar'. The higher you get and the further apart your legs are while airborne, the better.

Move completed ☐

The Windmill

Spin your arm in a continuous motion to play the chords on your 'guitar'.

Move completed ☐

On Your Knees!

Rock back and forth as if in prayer to a higher rock god.

Move completed ☐

Invent your own
Rock Stance

Place a picture of it here.
What is it called?
Write its name below

Dying Fly

Lie on your back and kick your legs in the air while playing and spinning on the spot.

Move completed ☐

Play With Your Teeth

Hold the 'guitar' up to your face and mime as if your teeth were plucking the strings.

Move completed ☐

At the same time you can check out these **Things You Wish You'd Invented**:
15: Tattoo • 25: Poetry • 35: CDs and DVDs • 42: School
67: Dancing • 75: Teenagers • 92: Vinyl Records

Prison

Being sent to prison is a common form of punishment today, but what did we do with criminals before prisons were invented?

In the Nick

There were plenty of punishments around before prisons, ranging from the expensive (paying a fine) to the horribly gruesome (having something chopped off – an ear, hand or nose, for example). The worst punishment was death – and still is in some parts of the world – and plenty of terrible ways to die were invented. Prisons in the ancient world were mostly used as places where accused criminals awaited trial, or convicted criminals awaited execution.

During the Middle Ages, people were sometimes locked up in castle dungeons. In Warwick Castle one group of soldiers was held in the dungeon for four years, but it wasn't a common punishment for ordinary prisoners.

In Britain in the 1700s, more than 200 crimes were punishable by death, which is one way of doing without prisons but seems a bit unfair. From the mid-1700s, people began to be locked up in prison as a punishment. Prisons were filthy and overcrowded, especially on the 'prison hulks' – huge prison ships – but conditions did improve over the 19th century and more emphasis was put on the rehabilitation of prisoners. Today there are 139 prisons in England and Wales holding nearly 80,000 prisoners. But people are still arguing about the effectiveness of this form of punishment.

 'Oubliettes' were pit-like castle dungeons with no windows and only a trapdoor on the ceiling. Prisoners could be thrown in and forgotten about, sometimes until they died ('oubliette' comes from the French word 'oublier' – to forget).

Prison Form

Once you have put this **Invention** to good use,
stick your Achieved Star here and fill in the form

Achieved

GET OUT OF THAT ONE!

Even the highest security prisons are not 100% secure. Can you match the following
escapologists to the prison they escaped from, when and what happened to them next?

THE GREAT ESCAPES

ESCAPEE

| Frank Morris | Jack Sheppard | Ronnie Biggs | Colonel Rose |
| Roger Bushell | Frank William Abagnale, Jr | Alfie 'Houdini' Hinds | Joseph 'Whitey' Riordan |

PRISON

| Newgate Prison | Stalag Luft III | Libby Prison | Alcatraz |
| Wandsworth Prison | Chelmsford Prison | Sing Sing Prison | Federal Detention Center |

LOCATION

| Central London, UK | San Francisco, California | Ossining, New York State | South-west London, UK |
| Essex, UK | Richmond, Virginia | Atlanta, Georgia | Zagan, Poland |

MORE DETAILS

| Escaped 3 times from the same prison | One of 3 escapees in a single murderous attempt | He escaped from the Old Bailey during his trial | Escaped through one of 3 tunnels named Tom, Dick and Harry |
| His final time in prison was for his part in the Great Train Robbery | One of 109 Union prisoners to escape during the American Civil War | He was a successful con artist and forger for 5 years, up to the age of 21 | His attempt was made into a film, starring Clint Eastwood |

YEAR

| 1724 | 1864 | 1941 | 1944 | 1957 | 1962 | 1965 | 1971 |

WHAT HAPPENED NEXT?

| Recaptured together with several had the other escapees, later ended in a doomed swap | Still believed he and his partners drowned in the escape bid but survived prison | Hanged – month were unable to make case, the court let them make attempt | Extensively the Nazis after being recaptured. Only 3 of the 76 escapees got to safety |
| Recaptured and sent to serve 8 years at Parkhurst Prison | Returned after being recaptured using bloodhounds. Got recaptured and died shortly during the escape | He spent 36 years on charges but was freed and decided Houdini | He pretended to be an undercover agent overseas being retained at a likelihood he was set |

At the same time you can check out these **Things You Wish You'd Invented**:
9: Money • 11: Fingerprinting • 12: Dynamite • 14: Playing Cards
15: Tattoo • 28: Lie Detector • 30: Magic • 65: Gunpowder • 101: Room 101

Planet Plastic

Plastic

Plastic is used in packaging, toys, furniture, computers, clothing ... just about everything! What on earth were things made of before it was invented?

Plastic Fantastic

There are natural plastics – cellulose is one type, found in cotton. But the first synthetic plastic wasn't invented until the twentieth century.

- In 1862 an English chemist called Alexander Parkes made a mixture of nitrocellulose (an explosive substance made from cellulose and nitric and sulphuric acids), and camphor. He called it Parkesine and it was used to make all sorts of domestic objects.
- In 1905 Leo Baekeland, a Belgian chemist working in New York, mixed phenol (a disinfectant) with formaldehyde (a preservative) and came up with Bakelite, the first completely man-made plastic, which could be moulded into any shape. It was used to make music recordings, telephones, furniture, radios and electrical insulation, among other things.
- During the 1920s and 30s, there were lots of important developments in the plastics industry: polythene was invented when an experiment went wrong at the plastics company ICI, nylon began to be used to make clothing, and neoprene (a synthetic rubber), vinyl and Perspex were invented.

Now it's hard to imagine life without plastic. It's useful stuff: light, inexpensive, extremely versatile and durable – and there lies the problem. Plastic is very difficult to get rid of because it takes so long to biodegrade. Rubbish tips all over the world are full of it.

Unfantastic plastic: It takes about 450 years for a plastic bottle to biodegrade! Recycling the same bottle can save enough energy to light a 60-watt light bulb for six hours and reusing plastic carrier bags could save millions of litres of oil a year.

Plastic **Form**

Once you have put this **Invention** to good use,
stick your Achieved Star here and fill in the form

Achieved

PLASTIC SURGERY

It can be a maze trying to sort the plastic for recycling because there are so many different types.
Recyclable plastic falls into seven categories – figure out which recycle group relates to which types
of plastic object, then help organise the recycling at home and school with your detailed knowledge!

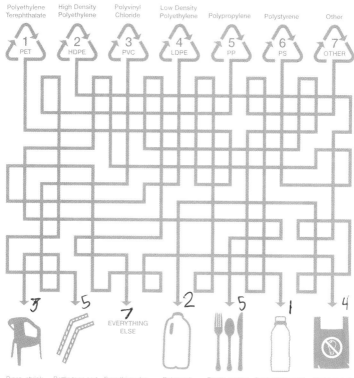

Polyethylene Terephthalate	High Density Polyethylene	Polyvinyl Chloride	Low Density Polyethylene	Polypropylene	Polystyrene	Other
1 PET	2 HDPE	3 PVC	4 LDPE	5 PP	6 PS	7 OTHER

3 — Pipes, shrink wrap, outdoor furniture

5 — Bottle tops and drinking straws

7 — EVERYTHING ELSE — Everything else that doesn't fall into the other six categories

2 — Detergent bottles and plastic milk bottles

5 — Plastic cutlery, take-away boxes, foam cups

1 — Drink bottles and plastic jars (like peanut butter jars)

4 — Bin bags and carrier bags

At the same time you can check out these **Things You Wish You'd Invented**:
2: Mobile Phone • 18: Fizzy Drinks • 32: Cutlery • 40: Spectacles • 53: Yo-yo
64: Umbrella • 77: Banana Suitcase • 86: Tin-Opener • 94: Flip Flops

Hot-Air Balloon

Flying machines were invented 120 years before the Wright brothers' plane made its first flight. They were quieter, more beautiful to look at and not nearly so bad for the environment. But they were a bit harder to steer ...

Up, Up and Away

Brothers Josef and Etienne Montgolfier came up with their invention after noticing that the hot air in an open fire made pieces of ash rise upwards. They didn't want to take any chances though: instead of going themselves, their first balloon-flight passengers in 1782 were a sheep, a cockerel and a duck, who flew successfully for 33 m over ten minutes. (The duck would have done better than that on its own.)

The first balloon flight with human passengers was made by Pilatre de Rozier and Francois d'Arlandes in Paris in 1783. Since the first balloons had a tendency to catch fire, the original idea was for condemned criminals to make the first flight. But Rozier and d'Arlandes decided to be brave and they made the journey themselves – without anything catching fire. Sadly Rozier was killed two years later when he tried to cross the Channel in a balloon.

Balloons have come a long way since 1782: they've soared as high as 34,000 m (in 1961), and travelled more than 40,000 km on a non-stop journey lasting 20 days (in 1999). The Channel, the Atlantic and even the Pacific have all been crossed successfully by hot-air balloon.

 Funky fuel: The fuel used for the Montgolfier brothers' first flight consisted of old boots and bad meat. No wonder they didn't fancy the trip themselves. Today's hot-air balloons are fuelled by propane, which isn't quite so smelly.

Hot-Air Balloon **Form**

Once you have put this **Invention** to good use,
stick your Achieved Star here and fill in the form

Achieved

———— MAKE YOUR OWN HOT-AIR BALLOON ————

You can make a simple indoor hot-air balloon. You need to be in a draughtless room with high ceilings.
It won't be able to take any passengers, but as it's not leaving the room that shouldn't matter!

———— WHAT YOU NEED ————

a small plastic bag, paper clips,
Sellotape, a hair dryer, a room
with a high ceiling, an assistant

Choosing your plastic bag

The best bags to make
into hot-air balloons are
thin ones (the thinner the
better). Carrier bags from
supermarkets are usually
thin enough. If you think
your bag is too big or you
think the handles might
get in the way, trim it down
from the top.

Checking your plastic bag

Take a look at your bag
and check for holes. Cover
the holes with Sellotape.
But be warned: the more
Sellotape you add to the
bag, the heavier your
balloon will be and it'll
take longer to float away.

Attaching the paper clips

Take several paper clips
and slip them around the
opening of your plastic
bag. This will help stabil-
ise it by countering the
weight of the balloon as it
fills with air. You may have
to experiment with the
number of clips you use:
not enough and the balloon won't rise steadily;
too many and the balloon will be too heavy and
won't fly at all!

HOLD HERE

Caution!

Take the hair dryer and
place it underneath the
bag (you will need some
help to hold the bag
upside down). Before
turning it on, make sure
the bag isn't touching the
hair dryer at any point, as
the heat may make the
plastic bag melt to the hair
dryer and it will be really
hard to remove.

Make it fly!

Now you're ready to
make your balloon fly.
Turn the hair dryer on
full and fill the bag
with hot air. The person holding on to the bag
should hold it lightly at the corners, and once
the balloon is ready to fly it should gently float
away from their fingers.

Trial and error

You may not get the perfect launch straight
away, but, with a few adjustments to the amount
of Sellotape or paper clips, you should be able
to send your balloon high up into the room.

Summarise the results of your first
attempted balloon flight here

At the same time you can check out these **Things You Wish You'd Invented:**
7: Time Zones • 20: Thermometer • 26: Submarine • 44: Helicopter
54: Steam Engine • 69: Weather Machine • 83: Parachute • 90: Maps

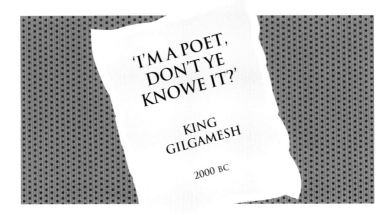

'I'M A POET, DON'T YE KNOWE IT?'

KING GILGAMESH

2000 BC

Poetry

Poetry has been around for thousands of years as a way of recording and expressing human experience through language. Simple rhyming and rhythmical verses are some of the first words we learn.

Prehistoric Poems

The oldest poetry wasn't written down at all. People told stories – made up or based on historical events – as poems, often very long ones. The words were remembered and passed on from generation to generation. The earliest written poems might well have been spoken aloud for centuries before they were written down.

The oldest surviving poem we know about is the *Epic of Gilgamesh*. It's from ancient Sumer – modern-day Iraq – and the earliest version dates from around 2000 BC. The poem is supposed to be about a real king, Gilgamesh of Uruk. Gilgamesh probably did exist, and reigned round about 2500 BC, but the things that happened to him in the poem are a little unlikely.

The ancient Greek epic poems, the *Iliad* and the *Odyssey*, are by a poet called Homer, though no one knows if he really existed. They were eventually written down around 700 BC. The *Iliad* tells the story of the war between the Greeks and Trojans, and the *Odyssey* is about Odysseus, a Greek hero, and his long journey home from the war. Like *Gilgamesh*, the subject of the poems have some basis in reality; the one-eyed giants, singing mermaids and sea monsters were probably all made up though.

The world's longest poem is the *Mahabharata*, an Indian epic poem sacred to the Hindu religion. It's about 1.8 million words long. One of the shortest poems in the world is by Charles Ghigna, called 'I', and it goes: Why?

Poetry **Form**

Once you have put this **Invention** to good use,
stick your Achieved Star here and fill in the form

Achieved

--- **RHYME TIME** ---

Take a look at the themes in the left-hand column and the three poetic forms below them.
Pick one theme and one form and see if you can write an original poem in the right-hand
column that fits your chosen theme and form.
When you've finished, mark your poem out of ten.

WRITE YOUR POEM TITLE HERE

--- THEME ---

A DREAM

MY BEST FRIEND

THE MOST
AMAZING INVENTION

THE VIEW FROM MY WINDOW

A HAPPY MEMORY

FLYING

WEATHER REPORT

--- FORM ---

HAIKU

A haiku consists of three unrhyming
lines. The first and third lines
must have five syllables, and the
second line seven syllables.

LIMERICK

A limerick tells a funny short
story in 5 lines, rhyming a a b b a.
The a-lines have 3 beats and the b-lines,
2 beats. They usually start something
like: 'There was a young lady/fellow
called/from _____'

ACROSTIC

An acrostic poem can be any
length, rhyming or non-rhyming,
but the first letter of each line can
be read down, spelling out a word or
message relating to the poem.

Mark your poem
out of ten

10

At the same time you can check out these Things You Wish You'd Invented:
19: Birthdays • 21: Guitar • 29: Post-It Notes • 42: School • 46: Music
50: Printing • 52: Language • 67: Dancing • 75: Teenagers

Submarine

People had been paddling about in boats for thousands of years before submarines were invented. Underwater travel proved a lot trickier to invent – even though fish make it look so easy.

Deep Down

- The first working submarine was built in 1620 by Cornelius Drebbel, a Dutch inventor employed by James I of England. We don't know exactly how it worked – it looks suspiciously like an upturned rowing boat and was powered by men pulling oars. A similar design had been drawn up by English naval officer William Bourne in 1578, but it was never made.
- The *Turtle*, built in 1775 by the American David Bushnell, was designed to sink a British warship. It failed, but it's the first military submarine and the first vessel we know about that could move and operate underwater.
- In 1864, the first submarine to sink a ship was the CSS H. L. Hunley, named after its designer. Unfortunately the submarine sank too.
- In 1870 Jules Verne's novel *Twenty Thousand Leagues Under the Sea* featured a submarine called *Nautilus* that inspired inventors to come up with more sophisticated machine-powered designs for submarines.
- In 1906 the first German U-boat was launched. During the First World War, U-boats proved very effective at sinking enemy ships. War at sea changed for ever and thousands of subs were used during the Second World War.
- In the 1950s new technology, including nuclear power, allowed submarines to remain underwater for months.

Submariners on today's nuclear subs spend weeks at a time in cramped conditions and without seeing the Sun. They often have 'coffin dreams' – they wake up convinced they're inside a coffin. True claustrophobia sufferers are rooted out during submarine training.

Submarine **Form**

Once you have put this **Invention** to good use,
stick your Achieved Star here and fill in the form

Achieved

DIVE! DIVE! DIVE!

It would be impossible for you to build your own working submarine, but you can
demonstrate one of the principles behind submarine engineering – buoyancy – in this
simple experiment. You can also check out the great films listed below featuring submarines.

WHAT YOU NEED

a plastic bottle (with cap), a straw, Blu-tack,
Sellotape, 7 x two-pence coins, elastic bands,
kitchen foil, a bathtub

WHAT TO DO

NOTE: YOU CAN REUSE THE BOTTLE
FROM THE THERMOMETER EXPERIMENT
(see **INVENTION** No. 20) AND SKIP TO 4

1. Cut a hole in the top of the bottle wide
enough for the straw to fit through.

2. Push the shorter end of the straw into
the bottle through the hole, as shown.

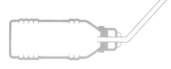

3. Take the Blu-tack and use it to seal the gaps
between the straw and the bottle top.

4. Make two holes in the side of the bottle, as
shown – they should be in line with each other.

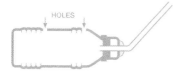

HOLES

5. Now take your coins: make one pile
of three coins and one of four coins.
Tape each pile up to secure the coins.

6. Place the pile of four coins to the
left of the lower of the two holes. Put a
rubber band around the pile to secure it.

7. Place the pile of three coins
to the left of the top hole. Put a
rubber band around the pile to secure it.

8. Next time you're in the bath,
remember to take your submarine
with you. Hold your creation underwater
so that it fills up with water. The end of
the straw should remain above water.

Your submarine will sink when full
of water. To make the submarine rise,
blow into the end of the straw.

SUBMARINE FEATURE FILMS

*20,000 Leagues
Under the Sea*
(1954) U

Das Boot
(1981) 12

*Raiders of the
Lost Ark* (1981) PG

The Abyss
(1989) 15

*The Hunt for Red
October* (1990) PG

*The Land That Time
Forgot* (1975) PG

*The League of
Extraordinary Gentlemen*
(2003) 12A

*The Life Aquatic with
Steve Zissou* (2004) 15

*The Spy Who
Loved Me* (1977) PG

Yellow Submarine
(1968) U

At the same time you can check out these Things You Wish You'd Invented:
8: Nuclear Weapons • 13: Satellite • 17: Morse Code • 20: Thermometer
24: Hot-Air Balloon • 44: Helicopter • 47: Radar • 54: Steam Engine • 90: Maps

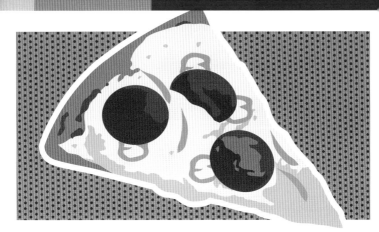

Pizza

People everywhere like pizza – there are hundreds of thousands of pizzerias around the world. But who invented it, when and where?

Pizza Premiere

Bread has been around for a very long time – at least 10,000 years. Ever since its invention, people have been adding toppings and tucking in. The ancient Greeks had a flat bread called *plakuntos* that they topped with onions and herbs and there were similar flat breads with toppings all over the Mediterranean.

The pizza we know and love today has a dough base made from water, flour and yeast topped with various ingredients, but the most basic, and the one that makes it a pizza, is tomato sauce. Tomatoes may not seem very exotic, but they come from America and were only introduced to Europe in the 1500s. At first people regarded tomatoes with suspicion and thought they were poisonous, but eventually they became popular. Towards the end of the 1700s in the area around Naples in southern Italy, people began to add tomato sauce to their local flat bread, and the pizza was born.

Although we don't know the culinary genius who first came up with this delicious snack, the world's first pizzeria is thought to be Antica Pizzeria in Naples, which opened in 1830 and is still going. It's only since the second half of the 20th century that pizza has become popular across the world as well as in Italy.

 Pizza Deluxe: The most expensive pizza in the world cost £2,150 and was made to raise funds for a charity in 2007. Toppings included caviar, champagne, lobster, venison, brandy and edible gold!

Pizza **Form**

Once you have put this **Invention** to good use, stick your Achieved Star here and fill in the form

Achieved

EATSA DA PIZZA

Making your own pizza is the best way for you to get exactly what you want, because you decide what goes on the pizza and in what quantity!

PIZZA BASE

You can either use a packet of pre-mixed ingredients (check the instructions carefully) or you can make your own from the following:
1/2 tbsp dried yeast, a pinch of salt, a pinch of caster sugar, 200 g plain flour, a dash of olive oil, 120 ml lukewarm water

1. To make your own base, sieve and mix together the yeast, salt, sugar and flour.

2. Make a well in the mixture and pour in the olive oil and water

3. Start mixing with a wooden spoon and then use your hands to knead the dough for about four minutes.

4. Roll out the dough and leave it to rise somewhere warm while you prepare your toppings! After about half an hour, your pizza dough is ready to dress ...

5. When your work of art is complete, put the pizza into a pre heated oven (220°C) and bake for 15–20 mins, or until the crust looks golden brown.

On the pizza below, draw the toppings you used. Here are some suggestions:

various cheeses, tomato, sundried tomato, spinach, egg, mushroom, pesto, aubergine, olives, pineapple, pepper (green, red and yellow), jalapenos, onion, chillies, sweetcorn, leek, garlic, asparagus, artichoke, ham, pepperoni, salami, sausage, bacon, chicken, anchovies, tuna, prawns

What is your pizza creation called?

Topping / Topping / Topping
Topping / Topping / Topping
Topping / Topping / Topping

At the same time you can check out these **Things You Wish You'd Invented:**
5: Fast Food • 18: Fizzy Drinks • 19: Birthdays • 20: Thermometer
32: Cutlery • 43: Sliced Bread • 68: Refrigerator • 79: Toothpaste

Honestly! I had nothing to do with the robbery!

Lie Detector

Some teachers and parents seem to have an uncanny ability to see through a lie, but they can never really know for certain – that would involve mind-reading! A polygraph machine can't mind-read either, but it has become known as a 'lie detector' because it is pretty good at picking up on the telltale signs of tall tales!

Ask No Questions, Hear No Lies …

If you tell a lie you'll probably feel a bit nervous about it. If it's a real whopper, your heart might start to pound and you might get a bit hot and sweaty. A polygraph machine is a device that monitors changes in the body that are associated with telling lies, such as blood pressure, heart rate, how sweaty you are and how fast you're breathing. These results are analysed.

US psychologist William M. Marston invented an early type of polygraph that measured blood pressure and was used in the First World War to question prisoners. Another psychologist, John A. Larson, invented a more modern type of polygraph in 1921 that was able to measure changes in a person's breathing and pulse rate too. Leonard Keeler, who worked with Larson, made further improvements in 1938 by adding a psychogalvanometer – a device that measures activity in the sweat glands.

But what if you're anxious, hot and sweaty for other reasons? Just the thought of taking a lie-detector test might worry you. Or what if you're really good at covering up stress? And polygraph results can be interpreted in different ways by different examiners. For these sorts of reasons, polygraphs are not foolproof and they can't be used as evidence in a law court in the UK.

 Wonder Man: William Marston, one of the inventors of the polygraph, also created the cartoon character Wonder Woman under his pen name Charles Moulton. Wonder Woman had a Lasso of Truth that forced anyone caught in it to be honest.

Lie Detector **Form**

Once you have put this **Invention** to good use,
stick your Achieved Star here and fill in the form

Achieved

IT'S ALL LIES!

They may be little white ones or massive whoppers, but the long and short of it is that everyone tells porky pies, although some people are better at lying than others. Use the tips below to try to catch someone out and uncover their web of deceit.

HOW TO SPOT A WHOPPER

It's impossible, unless you're a mind-reader, to know for certain if someone is telling the truth or lying, but here are some things to look out for which might give the game away:

TIP 1: Are they avoiding eye contact ... or making too much deliberate eye contact? | Have you seen through someone's lies this way? | y/n

TIP 2: Are they touching their face and hands more than usual? | Have you seen through someone's lies this way? | y/n

TIP 3: Do they appear nervous – for example, fidgeting a lot and looking uncomfortable? | Have you seen through someone's lies this way? | y/n

TIP 4: Are they slow to answer questions (perhaps stalling for time to invent their story)? | Have you seen through someone's lies this way? | y/n

TIP 5: Are they avoiding giving details ... or including an unusual amount of detail? | Have you seen through someone's lies this way? | y/n

TIP 6: Is their story inconsistent? Do they change certain details under intense questioning? | Have you seen through someone's lies this way? | y/n

TIP 7: Are they accusing you or someone else in order to cover up or deflect their lies? | Have you seen through someone's lies this way? | y/n

TIP 8: Are they refusing to answer your questions or trying to change the subject? | Have you seen through someone's lies this way? | y/n

---

YOU LIAR!

Name and shame the biggest liar you know!

Who among your family and friends lies the most?

What is the worst lie they've told?

How good at lying are they?

☐ Very good   ☐ OK   ☐ Terrible

How good at lying are YOU?

How many times have you caught them lying? | 0 0 0 | times

☐ Very good   ☐ OK   ☐ Terrible

At the same time you can check out these **Things You Wish You'd Invented:**
11: Fingerprinting • 22: Prison • 38: Sign Language
49: Homework Machine • 75: Teenagers • 88: Computer

The distinctive yellow colour of most Post-it notes is a registered trademark, as well as the name 'Post-it'

Post-It Notes

Post-it notes were invented by Arthur Fry, working for the company 3M, in 1974. By accident, a few years before, Fry's colleague Spencer Silver had discovered a very weak glue that was reusable and easily removed from paper without leaving a mark. Silver tried to think of a use for his seemingly useless glue, but couldn't.

Eventually, Arthur Fry came up with an idea for using the glue while he was at church one Sunday. He needed to mark his place in his hymnbook and thought how handy it would be if the bookmark stuck to the page but could then be removed easily. He developed the idea, and quickly discovered that Post-it notes were useful not only as bookmarks but for all sorts of other things too.

Post-its went on sale for the first time in 1980 and now you'll find them stuck all over the place. Since they're so useful, it seems strange that it took so long to come up with them.

Paper clips

If you use Post-it notes, you probably use paper clips too.

Johann Vaaler, who patented a paper clip design in 1899, is usually credited with their invention, but various forms of wire paper clip have been around since 1867.

The paper clip design we know today was patented by Henry Lankenau in 1934, although a very similar design called the Gem, which was never patented, has been around since the early 1890s.

Take note: In 1986, Andy Rourke, the bass guitarist in The Smiths, was sacked by Post-it note. It was left on his car windscreen by the lead singer. The note read: 'Andy, you have left The Smiths. Good luck and goodbye, Morrissey.'

Post-It Notes **Form**

Once you have put this **Invention** to good use,
stick your Achieved Star here and fill in the form

Achieved

... AND DON'T FORGET IT

Post-it notes help us to remember so many things that we would otherwise forget and get in
trouble for – and they've made our books and desks a lot more colourful. But here are a few other
things that your Post-it notes can be used for ...

POST-IT ART

Post-it notes are great for producing mini works
of art. The best thing is that you don't need nails
to hang your picture, just stick your art to the
wall in the safe knowledge that you won't ruin
the wallpaper when you take it down. Place your
favourite Post-it note here. A piece of art on
a Post-it note by artist R. B. Kitaj sold for £640 in
December 2000. Maybe you could sell yours ...

Place your Post-it here

How long did it
take you to draw?

What is the title of your Post-it note art?

How much do you
think it's worth?

POST-IT NAUGHTY

How sneaky are you? Try to stick a Post-it note to someone's back without them knowing ...

What did you write on the note?

I'm with stupid

Did you get
found out?

Did you get
into trouble?

THE POST-IT GAME

Elvis Presley

A game for two or more people. Give each player a Post-it note and
write the name of a famous celebrity on it without anyone else
seeing. When everyone has written down a name, stick your note to
the forehead of the person next to you.

Each person asks questions in turn to find out who is written on their
forehead. The other players can only answer 'yes' or 'no'. The player
who guesses the name on their Post-it in the fewest questions wins.

At the same time you can check out these **Things You Wish You'd Invented**:
14: Playing Cards • 16: Pencils • 25: Poetry • 39: Toilets and Toilet Paper • 46: Music
49: Homework Machine • 50: Printing • 71: Numbers • 99: Sticky Tape and Blu-tack

This is soooo demeaning!

Magic

Even though we all know it's a clever trick (well, most of us do), magic continues to entertain us, in theatres and on TV. But magic that makes you invisible and turns your enemies into toads has yet to be invented.

Hocus Pocus!

No one knows who was the first person to put a ball under a cup then make it vanish (one of the first magic tricks ever), but we do know that people were performing illusions in ancient civilisations all over the world. A piece of 4,000-year-old ancient Egyptian writing tells of the magician Dedi, who cut animals' heads off then miraculously put them back on – which sounds rather messy.

Performing illusions in Europe in the 16th century was a risky business because 'witches' were being executed for their magic powers. A helpful book called *The Discoverie of Witchcraft* by Reginald Scot explained how to tell the difference between magicians and real witches.

Many magicians performed in the streets, but by the 19th century they were appearing in theatres too, and magic acts were becoming more popular. Jean Eugène Robert-Houdin (1805–1871) is often called 'the father of modern magic' because of the many mechanical devices he invented to perform illusions. The early 20th century saw lots of astonishing new magicians, such as the escapologist Harry Houdini, and new magic tricks, such as Sawing a Woman in Half, invented by P. T. Selbit in 1921.

Algeria, 1856: A religious group called the Marabouts were using magic to incite a rebellion against the French, so the French government sent Robert-Houdin to discredit the Marabouts by performing much more impressive magic. It worked!

Magic Form

Once you have put this **Invention** to good use,
stick your Achieved Star here and fill in the form

Achieved

NOW THAT'S MAGIC!

Here is a cup and ball trick – one of the earliest types of magic trick we know about. All you need to impress
your friends is some scrunched-up paper balls, 3 plastic cups, a bit of practice and a lot of showmanship!

THE EFFECT

You will demonstrate a form of ancient magic by making a ball pass
mysteriously through the top of an upturned cup and appear underneath.

THE PERFORMANCE

1. Produce your three stacked plastic cups.
Explain to your audience that they are
ordinary cups (which they are).

2. Place the cups in front of you on the table
one at a time, counting them as you do so.

3. Place a single scrunched-up paper ball on top
of the middle cup (2). As you do this you should
keep up a patter to your audience – explain that
the cup and ball trick is one of the most
mysterious and ancient pieces of magic ...

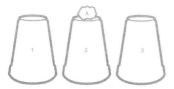

4. Stack cups 1 and 3 on to cup 2. Tell your audience
that the ancients had discovered a way to make
the material immaterial, and that you are going to
demonstrate this. Tap the top of the cups three times.

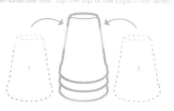

5. Finally, explain that the
ball will have magically
passed through the cup on
to the table top, lift up the
stack of cups to show the
ball underneath.

Now, that's magic!

THE SECRET

Before you perform this trick, you need to prepare another
paper ball and place this inside cup 2 before you stack the
cups. When you turn the cups over, turn them fast enough so
that the momentum keeps the paper in cup 2 from falling out
too soon. This way, and keeping your cup-holding hand
facing the audience, you should be able to disguise the fact
that a ball is already under cup 2 from the start. Your
audience will not see this ball until you reveal it at the end of
the trick (step 5). The great thing about this trick is that it is
already primed for you to repeat it, as paper ball A will end up
inside cup 2. You can do it time and time again!

At the same time you can check out these **Things You Wish You'd Invented:**
4: Cloning • 6: Photography • 10: Time Machine • 14: Playing Cards
19: Birthdays • 22: Prison • 49: Homework Machine • 71: Numbers • 85: Mirror

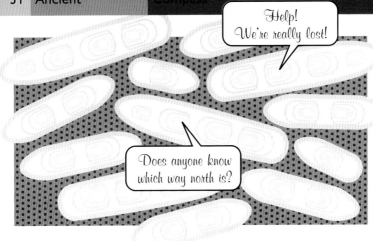

Compass

Before the compass was invented, life could be very tricky. Not only did people have to do without a reliable direction indicator, but they also had to do without street lights, torches, road maps and satellite navigation. This must have meant a lot of dark nights lost in the woods.

First Star on the Right ...

A compass uses a magnetised needle that aligns itself with the magnetic north of the Earth. It sounds simple, but people had to find their way without it for thousands of years.

- Around 200 BC, the Chinese used a magnetic metal pointer like a compass, but not for navigation: it was for working out lucky days for special events.
- But we do have the Chinese to thank for the earliest compass (well, probably): an early form of compass was used in China during the 11th century. It was a magnetic needle floating in a bowl of water.
- The more familiar form of a compass – a needle inside a box – appeared in Europe at the end of the 1200s. No one knows who invented it, or whether it came from a Chinese idea or was developed independently in Europe.

When it was clear, people used the stars to guide them at night. But of course lots of places tend to be a bit cloudy for at least some of the year. So the compass made getting about a lot easier. It also meant that people could explore new lands and have a much greater chance of getting home again. It's an invention we'd be lost without.

 Poles apart: The magnetic North Pole that compasses point to and geographical North Pole are very nearly the same but not quite – it's still good enough for most purposes, though. It's a very handy coincidence that they happen to be so close.

Compass Form

Once you have put this **Invention** to good use.
stick your Achieved Star here and fill in the form

Achieved

MAKE YOUR OWN COMPASS

Imagine being lost in the woods without any idea of how to get out. What you
need is a compass – but what if you don't have one? Here is a simple way to
make your own compass with the help of a few things you can find in your rucksack.

The most important part of any compass is the needle. Every compass needle points north
due to forces of magnetism caused by the Earth's molten iron core near the North Pole.

WHAT YOU NEED

a needle, a magnet, a cork, a bowl of water

if you don't have any of these,
you could try these alternative items:

Alternative needle:
a paper clip or nail

Alternative magnet:
silk or hair

Alternative cork:
a plastic bottle top

Alternative bowl of water:
a puddle

1. The first thing you need to do is turn your
needle (or piece of metal) into a magnet. The
easiest way to do this is by using a magnet.

Stroke the magnet down the length of the needle
about 30 times to make the needle magnetic. If
you have no magnet, you can stroke the needle
in one direction down your hair or a piece of silk
or synthetic material, but you'll have to stroke it
about 100 times to magnetise it.

2. Stick the needle through a small piece of cork
and place the cork in the centre of the bowl of
water, away from the sides.

3. You now have a very simple compass. Keep
the water as still as possible and your compass
in the centre of the water. You should find that
your compass, if properly magnetised. will turn
to the north/south position. depending which
pole is closer. Now you can escape from the
woods!

GET LOST

Have you ever been lost? Fill in the form below.

Have you ever been lost?

If yes, did you use a
compass to direct you?

Where did you get lost?

How long were
you lost for?

days   hours   mins

Write what happened in the space below

At the same time you can check out these **Things You Wish You'd Invented:**
1: Time • 13: Satellite • 26: Submarine • 34: Teleporter
44: Helicopter • 60. Inter-Stellar Travel • 90: Maps

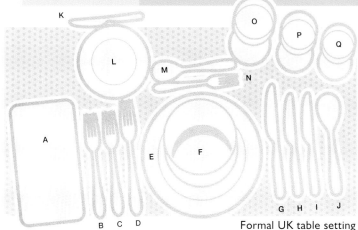

Formal UK table setting

Cutlery

Gnawing on bones looks so undignified. And how would you eat jelly without the invention of cutlery?

Knives, Foons and Sporks

Spoons were probably the first items of cutlery ever to be used. Back in the Stone Age, people started using shells to scoop up their food instead of using their fingers. Then someone had the bright idea of attaching a handle. Eventually spoons began to be made as one object, usually from wood.

Knives were around before spoons, but they were used as weapons or tools rather than cutlery. At some point in the past, it was realised that cutting up food was a lot less messy than tearing at it with your hands or teeth. Knives were used to cut things, then to stab them and put them in the mouth.

Forks hold food more securely than knives. They seem to have developed last, though some have been found dating from ancient Lydia (modern-day Turkey), ancient Greece and Rome. Forks didn't become popular until the Middle Ages and even then they were considered immoral and banned by the Church. Gradually they developed several tines (the first forks had just two), which became curved rather than straight. In the 19th century, sporks, combining the bowl of a spoon with the tines of a fork, were invented, as well as foons (like a spork but with the bowl facing the opposite way). You may have seen sporks provided with fast food, if not in your cutlery drawer!

 Spoonerisms galore: In 2002 the knirk was invented – a fork and a knife combined. The blade element might be dangerous, so the knirk has a safety device to stop users stabbing themselves. It's not proved popular.

Cutlery **Form**

Once you have put this **Invention** to good use,
stick your Achieved Star here and fill in the form

Achieved

--- **CUSTOMS AND ETIQUETTE** ---

Test your knowledge with the quiz below. Once you've completed it, memorise the correct
facts, then impress your friends to earn your star. Answers at the back of the book.

1. On the diagram opposite can you match
each item on the table setting to the
names below. Write the letter next to
the answer you think is correct.

☐ Red-wine glass ☐ Dessert spoon ☐ Butter knife

☐ Fish knife ☐ Napkin ☐ Dinner plate

☐ Dinner fork ☐ Salad knife ☐ Water glass

☐ Dinner knife ☐ White-wine glass ☐ Fish fork

☐ Salad fork ☐ Dessert fork ☐ Soup spoon

☐ Bread plate ☐ Soup bowl

2. What is unusual about the French
table setting?

a) You have a choice of five wine
glasses to choose from
b) The fork is placed with the tips
facing down on the table
c) Napkins are not provided
d) The soup bowl has a hole in it

3. In Portugal, which of the following is
correct behaviour as a guest in
someone's house?

a) To remain standing until you are told to
sit down
b) To take your shoes off before entering
the house
c) To wash your hands as soon as you
arrive
d) To smash a plate

4. In Italy, before eating spaghetti,
what is it incorrect to do?

a) Add Parmesan before tasting it
b) Take a drink
c) Add salt before tasting it
d) Cut it up

5. In Peru, what is offered before the
meal to *Pachamama* (Mother Earth)?

a) A few coins
b) A sip of beer
c) A sacrificial goat
d) A girl from the local village

6. What is it perfectly acceptable to do
in Japan when eating hot noodles?

a) Spit
b) Slurp
c) Burp
d) Talk

7. What is frowned upon in many
countries, including China, Japan,
India, Malaysia and Pakistan?

a) Eating with your left hand
b) Eating with your right hand
c) Drinking with your left hand
d) Drinking with your right hand

8. In Afghanistan, what will the host
do during a meal?

a) Eat more food than his guests
b) Eat less food than his guests
c) Eat exactly the same amount of
food as his guests
d) Eat nothing at all

At the same time you can check out these Things You Wish You'd Invented:
5: Fast Food • 18: Fizzy Drinks • 19: Birthdays • 23: Plastic
43: Sliced Bread • 66: Tea • 86: Tin-Opener • 97: Alcoholic Drinks

Battery

Today, batteries are useful if you can't plug something into an outlet, but when they were first invented they were the only things capable of generating an electric current.

A Bright Spark

Alessandro Volta was born in 1745, when people used candles to light their homes and no one knew what electricity was. He worked as a physicist and, in 1775, he invented a machine that could produce and store static electricity, which he generated by rubbing cat fur across a metal plate.

Volta's most famous invention came about because of frogs' legs rather than cat fur. In 1780 a doctor called Luigi Galvani noticed that dissected frogs' legs twitched when they were brought into contact with two different metals. Galvani thought that this was due to 'animal electricity'. Volta realised that the electricity was due to the metal and had nothing to do with the dead frog. He began experimenting and discovered that some metals could generate an electric current if they were submerged in acid. In 1800 he invented the 'voltaic pile', the first ever battery, made from copper and zinc strips separated by paper soaked in salt water and submerged in diluted sulphuric acid. He had worked out a way of generating an electric current.

Volta's battery was the first portable source of energy and without it radio, telegraph and electric light, among other things, wouldn't have been possible.

Special powers: Napoleon was so impressed with Volta's invention that, in 1801, he invited him to Paris to lecture the French National Institute. He congratulated Volta and even took part in his experiments during the lecture. Later he made Volta a count.

Battery **Form**

Once you have put this **Invention** to good use,
stick your Achieved Star here and fill in the form

Achieved

I HAVE THE POWER!

Did you know it's possible to make your own battery using things you can find around the house?

EXPERIMENT ONE

For experiment one you'll need 4 LEMONS (the bigger the better), 4 TWO PENCE COINS, 4 TWO-INCH NAILS (most nails are coated in ZINC), COPPER WIRE and an LED (Light Emitting Diode). The copper wire, nails and LED can be found in a hardware shop.

In a normal battery, a chemical reaction occurs in the acidic solution within the battery when a circuit is made. In this case the lemon will act as the solution, the nail will be the negative terminal and the coin will be the positive terminal.

Insert a nail in one end of a lemon and a coin in the other: you now have a very basic battery. Unfortunately there is not enough power in this 'battery' to light an LED: you need to repeat the instructions above another three times to make four batteries.

Once you've made your four batteries, attach them together with the copper wire as shown in the diagram below. Connect a negative nail terminal to a positive coin terminal on another lemon, and repeat until you have them all joined together with wire, leaving a wire at each end of your lemon line, yet to be connected.

Take an LED and attach the wires to it as shown and it should light up. The LED also has positive and negative terminals too, so make sure you get it the right way round – the negative terminal on the LED has a flat area on the wire just under the bulb. This time you are going to connect the negative nail terminal in the lemon to the LED's negative terminal, and the positive coin terminal in the other lemon to the LED's positive terminal. Congratulations – you've made a battery using fruit!

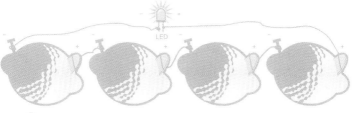

EXPERIMENT TWO

You can also make a battery from vinegar! The vinegar will act in the same way the lemon did in the experiment above. Take an empty plastic container (a tub for camera film is perfect) and pour in some vinegar. Insert the nail through the top of the lid, then do the same with the copper wire (as shown). Now this one actually looks more like a battery than the lemon did. Again, one vinegar battery is not enough to power an LED, so make three or four and attach them together as you did with the lemon battery.

It is possible to power a low current calculator with just a few vinegar batteries. Rather than hooking the batteries to an LED, attach two vinegar batteries together, remove the calculator battery and attach the vinegar batteries with wire to the positive and negative terminals in the calculator, where the regular battery would have been connected. You should now be able to continue your maths homework!

At the same time you can check out these **Things You Wish You'd Invented**:
2: Mobile Phone • 6: Photography • 8: Nuclear Weapons • 54: Steam Engine
81: Laser • 86: Tin-Opener • 88: Computer • 100: Chindogu

Teleporter

Have you ever wished you could say 'Beam me up, Scottie!' and be instantly transported to wherever you wanted to go?

Energise!

There's no doubt that a teleporter – a device that can transport anything instantly over any distance – would be one of the most brilliant inventions ever, if only someone had got round to inventing it. No more waiting for buses in the pouring rain, no more sitting in traffic jams. Think of all the time you'd save for more important things.

However, the chances of someone inventing a real teleporter seem pretty remote. Somehow, you'd have to work out a way of converting every atom of a person or thing into a stream of fast-moving energy, find a way of directing that energy wherever you wanted it to go, then rearrange all the atoms exactly as they were to start off with at the destination (otherwise you might end up with an ear in the middle of your face).

On the other hand ... physicists are currently researching 'quantum teleportation', which relies on a strange phenomenon in which two particles can be co-related, so that if one behaves in a certain way, the same thing happens to the other, no matter how far apart they are. One day this spooky-sounding science could be used to communicate and even to create copies of the particles at remote destinations.

 To boldly go where no man has gone before: Teleporters were invented back in the 1960s ... in the TV series *Star Trek*. The programme's 'matter transporter' was used countless times to remove the main characters from perilous situations.

Teleporter **Form**

Once you have put this **Invention** to good use,
stick your Achieved Star here and fill in the form

Achieved

---------------------------------- **GET ME OUT OF HERE!** ----------------------------------

Unlike a time machine (see **Invention** No. 10) you can't travel through time with a teleporter,
you can only travel from one place to another in the present. Which situations have you wished
you could be teleported to or away from? List six times when you wished you could disappear.
e.g. an embarrassing moment, a boring family function, or a telling-off.

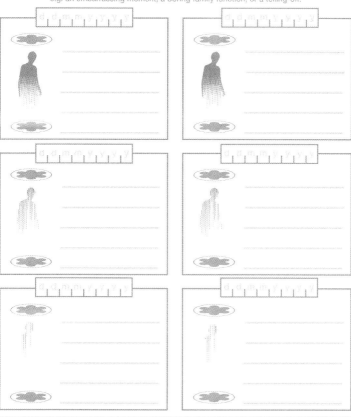

 At the same time you can check out these **Things You Wish You'd Invented:**
1: Time • 7: Time Zones • 10: Time Machine • 13: Satellite • 30: Magic
31: Compass • 60: Inter-Stellar Travel • 90: Maps

CDs and DVDs

Only a hundred years ago, listening to music was a rather complicated business and watching moving images was completely impossible.

Sound and Vision

- In 1877 Thomas Edison invented the phonograph – the first machine to record sound. Ten years later, Emile Berliner invented the gramophone, which recorded sound on to a zinc disc, and eventually on to vinyl.
- In 1926 John Logie Baird, famous for inventing television, invented a machine that recorded video on to a wax disc. He called it Phonovision.
- Many people were frustrated by the sound quality of vinyl records and their lack of durability. By 1970 scientist James Russell had developed a way of digitally encoding information, including sounds, on to a disc, read by a laser. Sony eventually licensed this technology.
- At the same time, Klass Compaan and Piet Kramer, working for the Dutch company Philips, came up with a prototype glass disc that could record video. But the idea didn't take off for another 20 years.
- Throughout the 1970s, Sony and Philips worked to perfect CD technology. They collaborated to come up with a standard that was demonstrated in public in 1979 and went on sale in 1982.
- In the 1990s Digital Versatile Discs for recording video were developed, based on Compaan's and Kramer's invention. Even though they're the same size, DVDs can store much more information than CDs.
- DVDs went on sale in Japan in 1996, and in North America and Europe in the following two years. They very quickly replaced video tapes.

Playtime: Akio Morita, head of Japanese company Sony, insisted that CDs should have a playing time of at least 74 minutes because that's how long it takes to play his favourite piece of music: Beethoven's 9th symphony.

CDs and DVDs **Form**

Once you have put this **Invention** to good use,
stick your Achieved Star here and fill in the form

Achieved

SOUNDTRACK OF YOUR LIFE TITLE HERE

What is the name of your CD soundtrack? Write the name of your album in the spine below

7 243 8 59211 5

YOUR SOUNDTRACK

Take a typical week in your life and make your own 'soundtrack to your life' album mix.
Write down the songs that describe your week below. Some suggestions for moments in
your week have been made to get you on track, but you don't have to use them if your
songs don't fit. Make a copy of your soundtrack and add it to your music collection.

Life moment 1
Waking up

Track and artist

Life moment 2
Getting ready for
a Monday morning

Track and artist

Life moment 3
Maths lesson

Track and artist

Life moment 4
Art lesson

Track and artist

Life moment 5
Getting your marks

Track and artist

Life moment 6
The weekend is here

Track and artist

Life moment 7
Going round to
your best friend's

Track and artist

Life moment 8
In the town

Track and artist

Life moment 9
Sunday evening

Track and artist

Life moment 10
A new week is about

Track and artist

At the same time you can check out these **Things You Wish You'd Invented:**
19: Birthdays • 21: Guitar • 46: Music • 56: World Wide Web • 67: Dancing
75: Teenagers • 78: Language Decoder • 81: Laser • 88: Computer

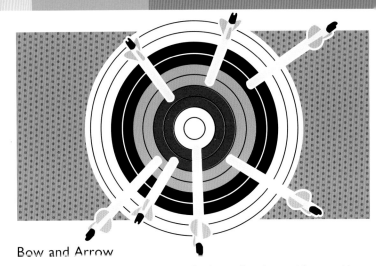

Bow and Arrow

If you lived ten thousand years ago, a dead animal might provide you with food, clothing, tools (bones or antlers), string (tendons), and perhaps a bag (stomach). Animals were so useful when dead that an effective means of killing them was high on the agenda.

Ancient Archery

Using a bow and arrow, people could kill animals that were quite far away with a minimum of fuss and effort. There is evidence to suggest they have been used in many areas of the world for tens of thousands of years.

- The bow and arrow had been invented in Africa by around 30,000 BC – they're shown in cave paintings from that date.
- By around 18,000 BC flint was used to make deadly arrow heads.
- The oldest bow ever found was discovered in a bog in Holmgaard, Denmark. It's 1.5 m long, made from elm and beautifully designed using 8,000-year-old technology.
- The 5,000-year-old mummy found in the Alps, Otzi the Iceman, had been shot by an arrow and was carrying a bow made of yew. Bows and arrows had been used in warfare long before that.
- During the Middle Ages the longbow became the most feared weapon on the battlefield. It was as tall as the archer, who had to be very strong and skilled to fire it. An arrow shot from a longbow could travel up to 400 m!
- Guns replaced bows and arrows as weapons of war from the 1500s.

Crossbows fire arrows mechanically. They were first used in China and Greece around 2,500 years ago, and were used in warfare until the Middle Ages. Though very powerful, they were slow to fire and expensive to make.

Bow and Arrow **Form**

Once you have put this **Invention** to good use,
stick your Achieved Star here and fill in the form

Achieved

TARGET PRACTICE

You need a great aim to go hunting with a bow and arrow. The best thing to do is practise, practise, practise, and all you need for that are five empty tin cans, a tennis ball and a friend to make the whole thing more exciting as a competition.

READY

Set up five empty tin cans ...

AIM

... and practise your aim by trying to knock them over with a tennis ball.

FIRE!

Take one shot at each can. Reset them and give your friend a go. You should both attempt to get all five cans down five times. Jot down your scores as you go, marking your cards with a tick for a hit and a cross for a miss. At the end, count up your overall score to see who's got the best aim.

SCORECARD

YOUR SCORECARD

1	2	3	4	5

OVERALL TOTAL (out of 25) | 0 | 0 |

SCORECARD

YOUR FRIEND'S SCORECARD

1	2	3	4	5

OVERALL TOTAL (out of 25) | 0 | 0 |

 At the same time you can check out these **Things You Wish You'd Invented:**
8: Nuclear Weapons • 22: Prison • 40: Spectacles • 47: Radar
65: Gunpowder • 86: Tin-Opener

Fashion

You probably have a finely developed sense of what's fashionable and what isn't. Your granny's fashion sense is no less keen than yours – it just happens to date from another era. But has fashion always been around?

Fashion Victims

It's likely that the first people to wear clothes mainly cared about keeping warm – this was especially crucial during the Ice Age. Later on, clothing became important as a way of showing class, status, wealth and occupation as well as keeping warm and covered up. Until the 20th century, most people didn't have very much choice about what they could wear – clothes weren't mass-produced, so most things had to be handmade and, unless you were really rich, that was probably your job or your mum's. But if you did happen to be dead posh, the clothing you wore was a way of telling everyone about it. And that's how fashion began.

In some societies, the upper classes were worried about people who were rich but not properly posh: if they looked upper class because they wore expensive clothes, who was to tell they weren't? So 'sumptuary laws' were made to stop ordinary people with spare cash from wearing certain fashions! There were laws like this in ancient Rome and medieval England. Today, however, most people don't care whether you're posh or not, or even how much money you have. So it's possible to be common and broke and still be fashionable. Hooray!

Big-bottomed beauty: One of the strangest fashions ever must be the bustle. It was popular with ladies in Victorian England from the mid- to late-1800s, and consisted of a special framework designed to make bottoms stick out more.

Fashion **Form**

Once you have put this **Invention** to good use,
stick your Achieved Star here and fill in the form

Achieved

—— DEDICATED FOLLOWER OF FASHION ——

In the spaces below, build up a fashion portfolio with photos or drawings
of your favourite outfits (and, if you dare, some of the worst ones too!).

Your favourite outfit	Your favourite pair of shoes	Your poshest outfit

Why you like it	Why you like them	Good posh or bad posh?

Your worst Christmas present	Your worst jumper	Your worst outfit ever!

Why you hate it	Why you hate it	What were you thinking?

At the same time you can check out these **Things You Wish You'd Invented:**
6: Photography • 15: Tattoo • 19: Birthdays • 40: Spectacles • 42: School
45: Jeans • 51: Make-up • 62: Bling • 75: Teenagers • 80: Silk • 85: Mirror

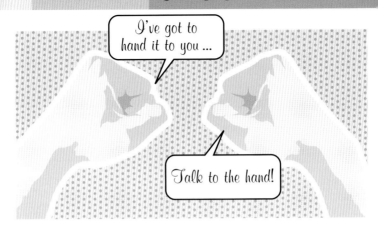

Sign Language

Our need to communicate is part of what makes us human. So the invention of a standard sign language was pretty essential for millions of people.

Silent Speaking

For anyone who can't hear or speak, making signals with the hands and body is the only way of communicating, unless you want to write everything down or have access to a keyboard all the time. Before the invention of a standard sign language, deaf and mute people invented their own. We'll never know, but perhaps our ancestors used a form of sign language before humans developed speech – or used it if they were out hunting and didn't want to make a sound, or needed to communicate with a different tribe.

If a group of people get together and invent their own sign language, it's not going to be understood by anyone who hasn't learned it. Standardised sign languages have been used since the 1600s. The first ones were developed in Italy and France as a way of improving education for deaf people. In 1755 Abbé de l'Épée set up the first free school for the deaf and helped to develop a system of signed communication which forms the basis of French Sign Language today, and influenced many other international sign languages. Even so, different countries have different sign languages just as they have different spoken languages. British Sign Language, Irish Sign Language and American Sign Language are all very different, even though English is the common spoken language.

 Some hearing-impaired people can lip-read. It can be hard to distinguish different words: author Henry Kisor wrote a book about his experiences called *What's That Pig Outdoors?*, which was how he'd interpreted the question, 'What's that big loud noise?'

Sign Language **Form**

Once you have put this **Invention** to good use,
stick your Achieved Star here and fill in the form

Achieved

TALKING WITH YOUR HANDS

Certain gestures, such as a thumbs up for 'OK', can cross language barriers and aren't only used by
people with hearing difficulties. If you don't already know any, why not learn some sign language
and take talking with your hands a step further?

GIVE ME A SIGN

Try your hand at the following words and phrases. Can you match each diagram
to the phrase being signed? Try them out on someone to earn your star.

1. Hello / Goodbye • 2. Sorry • 3. Love • 4. Please • 5. How are you? • 6. Thank you

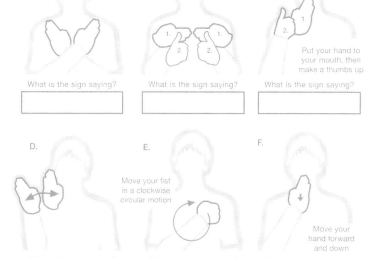

A.

What is the sign saying?

B.

What is the sign saying?

C.

Put your hand to
your mouth, then
make a thumbs up

What is the sign saying?

D.

What is the sign saying?

E.

Move your fist
in a clockwise
circular motion

What is the sign saying?

F.

Move your
hand forward
and down

What is the sign saying?

At the same time you can check out these **Things You Wish You'd Invented**:
11: Fingerprinting • 17: Morse Code • 28: Lie Detector • 52: Language
67: Dancing • 74: Braille • 78: Language Decoder • 96: Know-It-All Hat

Toilets and Toilet Paper

Life without flushing toilets simply doesn't bear thinking about, does it?

Flushed with Success

Toilets have been discovered from nearly 5,000 years ago, but the world's oldest flushing loos are the ones at the Minoan palace of Knossos on Crete, which are 4,000 years old. Ancient Minoan royalty sat on a wooden seat over a clay bowl, which was flushed with water flowing through pipes and into stone sewers.

3,600 years later, the UK's first flushing toilet was invented by John Harrington, Queen Elizabeth I's godson. In 1597 he installed one in his godmother's palace at Richmond. The Queen was pleased with it but banished Harrington from court for writing a rude essay about it.

Harrington's toilet wasn't commonly used until the late 1700s, when Alexander Cumming invented the 'S' bend. Cumming took out the first patent on a modern toilet, which was improved upon by Joseph Bramah in 1778.

The House of Lords in London still has an original Bramah loo, and it's still being used.

> **On a Roll**
>
> Toilet paper has probably been used since the invention of paper. The earliest record of it is in 14th-century China.
>
> The first paper to be made and sold exclusively for using in the loo was made by Joseph Gayetty and went on sale in the USA in 1857 as 'Gayetty's Medicated Paper'.
>
> Before toilet paper people used all sorts of things, including moss, leaves, corncobs and shells.
>
> Very rich people have used materials like wool and even lace.

Veni vidi wee-wee: Ancient Roman public toilets really were public – people used a multi-seated toilet without dividing walls or doors. And what's more, these loos were unisex, and could seat up to 100 men and women.

Toilets and Toilet Paper **Form**

Once you have put this **Invention** to good use,
stick your Achieved Star here and fill in the form

Achieved

— TOILET HUMOUR —

Test your knowledge with the quiz below. Once you've completed it, memorise the
correct facts, then impress your friends to earn your star. Answers at the back of the book.

1. In 1391, the first toilet paper was used
   by a Chinese emperor, but how big
   were the sheets?

a) Tiny – postage stamp size
b) The same size as today's paper
c) Big – equivalent to A4 paper
d) Massive – 60 x 90 cm

2. What caused the smell during the
   'Great Stink' in London in 1858?

a) Untreated sewage in the street
b) Air pollution from factories
c) Untreated sewage in the Thames
d) A rat infestation

3. Which of the following statements
   is FALSE? Before the invention of
   toilet paper ...

a) Hawaiians used coconut shells
b) Eskimos used snow
c) Romans used their hands
d) Early Americans used corncobs

4. In the middle ages, before the invention
   of toilets in the home, where did the
   waste from chamber pots go? Was it ...

a) Hidden in the closet?
b) Collected once a week?
c) Thrown out of the window?
d) Buried in the garden?

5. On average, how much time do people
   spend on the loo over a lifetime?

a) 2 years
b) 3 years
c) 4 years
d) 5 years

6. When is World Toilet Day?

a) 13 January
b) 2 June
c) 19 November
d) Every day

7. On average, how often does a
   person visit the toilet in a year?

a) 1,500 times
b) 2,500 times
c) 4,500 times
d) 6,500 times

8. Where does the word 'toilet'
   come from?

a) It has English origins and means
   'to let go of oneself'
b) It has Chinese origins and means
   'to remove oneself from public view'
c) It has French origins and means 'the
   act of dressing and preparing oneself'
d) It has German origins and means
   'the act of washing oneself'

9. What is toilet humour?

a) Jokes passed between people
   in toilet cubicles
b) Practical jokes played on people
   in the toilet
c) Jokes or comments directed
   at bodily functions
d) All of the above

10. There are many names for the toilet,
    but can you spot the made-up
    one below?

a) House of Honour
b) John
c) Throne Room
d) Passing Place

At the same time you can check out these Things You Wish You'd Invented:
48: Aspirin • 63: Anaesthetics • 79: Toothpaste • 91: Antibiotics • 95: Soap

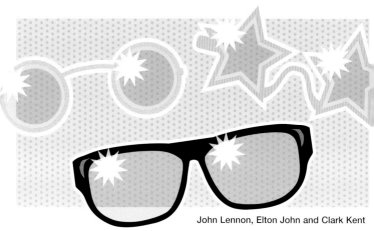

John Lennon, Elton John and Clark Kent

Spectacles

Before spectacles were invented, short- or long-sighted people had to get very close to objects or very far away to see them. Or just live in a blur.

Perfect Vision

Looking through a lens to make something small appear bigger has been going on for thousands of years. The ancient Egyptians made lenses as early as 2600 BC. The short-sighted Roman playwright, Seneca, looked through a glass globe of water in order to read books. During the Middle Ages, myopic monks looked at books through pieces of glass they called 'reading stones'. But it was a while before anyone had the idea of strapping them to people's heads.

No one really knows who invented specs, but in the 1200s the Fransiscan friar Roger Bacon was the first person to write about lenses and how they could be used to correct sight. There's no evidence that he made any specs, though. The first pair probably appeared in Italy around 1300.

The earliest glasses had to be held in front of the eyes or balanced precariously on the nose. A rigid bridge wasn't invented until the 1600s and the first spectacles with side pieces that went over the ears to stop them falling off all the time didn't appear until about 1750.

> **Life through a Lens**
>
> The first wearable contact lenses were made in 1887 by Adol Eugen Fick – they covered the whole eyeball, not just the area around the pupil, and were extremely uncomfortable.
>
> In 1936 William Feinbloom used plastic to make contact lenses easier to wear.
>
> During the 1950s and 60s contact lenses became lighter and thinner, and the first soft lenses became available in 1971.

A **monocle is a circular lens** for one eye only, kept in place by the eye socket. They became fashionable for wealthy men in the late 19th century. Famous monocle-wearers of more recent years include astronomer Sir Patrick Moore and former boxer Chris Eubank.

Spectacles **Form**

Once you have put this **Invention** to good use,
stick your Achieved Star here and fill in the form

Achieved

—MAKE 3-D GLASSES —

WHAT YOU NEED:
a photocopier, scissors, glue,
blue cellophane, red cellophane

1. Photocopy this page and cut out the glasses around the solid black line. Then cut out the eye holes, following the dotted lines. Use this as a template to draw around on a piece of thick card, then cut out your sturdier pair. This pair of 3-D glasses may be too small for you. You may need to increase the size of the template.

2. Cover the right eyehole with a piece of blue cellophane, and the left eyehole with a piece of red cellophane. Secure the cellophane on the back of the card with glue or Sellotape.

3. Now test your glasses on the pictures of Trafalgar Square and Nelson's Column below.

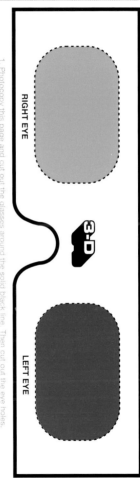

RIGHT EYE

3-D

LEFT EYE

At the same time you can check out these **Things You Wish You'd Invented:**
23: Plastic • 37: Fashion • 50: Printing • 59: Glass • 61: Microscope and Telescope
62: Bling • 72: X-ray • 81: Laser • 84: Anti-Ageing Pills

Football

Love it or hate it, football has had enough fans to keep it in the premier league of the world's most popular sports for many, many years.

Match of the Day

People have been kicking balls around for thousands of years, so it's impossible to say who invented football or when.

- The ancient Egyptians, Greeks and Romans all played football games.
- An early form of football called cuju was played in ancient China about 2,500 years ago. Two teams of twelve players competed to kick a leather ball through a total of twelve goals. In Japan, Kemari was played from about AD 600. It was a bit like a keepie-uppie competition.
- During the Middle Ages in England, huge football games were played between entire villages, in which players tried to kick a blown-up pig's bladder into the opposing team's church. It's thought that the game we know today as football originated in these riotous matches.
- Football began to be played in public schools in England from the 1500s onwards. Rules were made so that matches could be played between schools and the game gradually evolved into the sport we know today.
- The first football clubs were set up in England in the 19th century, and the Football Association, founded in 1863, established a universal set of rules for the game. The first match of Association Football was between Barnes and Richmond (in south-west London). It ended in a goalless draw.

Football phobia: Edward II banned football in London in 1314 because it caused noise and disruption and 'many evils'. In 1349 Edward III also banned football, because he thought everyone should practise archery instead.

Football **Form**

Once you have put this **Invention** to good use,
stick your Achieved Star here and fill in the form

Achieved

GOOOOAAAAAALLLLLL!!!

Prove your footballing credentials by filling out the form below. To earn your star you must win a
penalty shoot-out. Or if kicking a ball around isn't your idea of fun, but bossing people around is,
why not try your hand at management instead?

PENALTY!

Hold a penalty shoot-out with a mate and record
the outcome below. Toss a coin to decide who
gets to choose whether to start in goal or take
the first penalty.

If a goal is scored, colour in the relevant star; if
not, leave it blank. Then it's the other person's
turn and the goalie becomes the penalty-taker.
Keep taking turns until you have both taken
five penalties each. The winner is the person
who has scored the most goals.

Player one

Penalties scored

☆ ☆ ☆ ☆ ☆

Player two

Penalties scored

☆ ☆ ☆ ☆ ☆

Draw balls to show where the penalties went in

If you didn't win the first time, how
many times did it take until you did win?

STRATEGY!

Organise a friendly match between your mates.
It is your job to manage one of the teams.
Before the game, plan out some goal-scoring
moves for your team, using the diagram below.
Make sure your team know what to do to seal
victory!

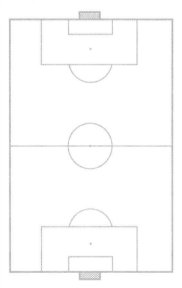

Did your
team win?   What was the
final score?

Did your planned moves work?

At the same time you can check out these **Things You Wish You'd Invented:**
9: Money • 15: Tattoo • 31: Compass • 42: School
75: Teenagers • 82: Skateboard • 88: Computer • 101: Room 101

MUST TRY HARDER

School

Whether you love school or hate it, it's quite handy to be able to read, write and maybe even do some basic maths. You have to admit, we're all better off with a bit of book learnin'.

Top of the Class

Back in the days before school dinners, children learned from their parents. In the very beginning, subjects included Hunting, Gathering, and Food Poisoning and How to Avoid It. Later, Farming and Keeping Animals joined the curriculum. Formal education came later ...

- The first schools were in ancient Egypt, around 3000 BC, and were for boys from rich families who would become scribes (professional writers – few people could read and write), priests or government officials.
- In ancient India, teachers called Gurukuls ran schools that taught subjects including philosophy and medicine. The schools were free, but richer families paid a contribution when the child had finished his or her studies.
- The ancient Romans had private schools for the rich, where children (mainly boys) were taught to read and write in Greek and Latin, and arithmetic.
- Schools were set up in Europe during the Middle Ages, often by the Church or by guilds – associations of skilled workers – who would teach their trade.
- The Education Act of 1870 provided compulsory state-funded schooling for all children aged between 5 and 13 in England and Wales. Before that, unless they could afford to pay, few children went to school at all.

 Learning the hard way: School for ancient Egyptian scribes was tough. One teacher wrote in a sort of school rules book, 'pass no day in idleness or you will be beaten'. Teachers were still beating pupils in the UK until the late 20th century!

School **Form**

Once you have put this **Invention** to good use,
stick your Achieved Star here and fill in the form

Achieved

SCHOOL REPORT CARDS

Every term your school will write reports on you. Isn't it time you
had the chance to turn the tables and write a report on your school?

Name of your school

Date

Mark the following: A, B, C, D or F *

State of buildings

General facilities

School hours

Teachers

School dinners

Extra-curriculum activities

Uniform (if applicable)

Discipline

Sport facilities

Overall

* A – Excellent, B – Above average, C –
Average, D – Below average, F – Fail

List the best things about your school

List the worst things about your school

What is your least favourite subject?

Why?

How could this lesson be improved?

What is your average grade?   Do you think this is fair?

How would you assess the level of homework you get?

Too much   Too little   Just right

How much freedom do you get in and out of class?

Too much   Too little   Just right

What is the main thing you would you like to see changed in your school?

Give your school a final percentage mark   0 0 0 %

At the same time you can check out these **Things You Wish You'd Invented**:
16: Pencils • 37: Fashion • 41: Football • 49: Homework Machine
52: Language • 71: Numbers • 75: Teenagers • 88: Computer • 101: Room 101

Sliced Bread

You often hear things referred to as 'the best thing since sliced bread'. But when was sliced bread invented, and why is it such a good thing?

Bread: Who Kneads It?

You wouldn't have thought that inventing a machine to slice bread would be that difficult. Yet one man spent 16 years of his life on the project: Otto Rohwedder worked tirelessly to save everyone the effort of using a bread knife. In 1917 a fire destroyed his prototype slicer after five years' work and he still didn't succeed in inventing a bread-slicing machine until 1928. The problem wasn't slicing the bread but keeping it fresh once it had been sliced. Rohwedder's machine sliced the bread then immediately wrapped it up to keep it fresh. The first pre-sliced bread went on sale in Missouri, USA, in 1928.

Cutting your own bread isn't always easy, depending on the shape of the bread and the sharpness of the knife, so ready-sliced bread is pretty handy. Within five years of Rohwedder's invention, 80% of bread sold in the USA was sliced.

Pop-up Toasters

The easy way to make toast requires sliced bread and a pop-up toaster, which had handily been invented first. The first electric toaster was invented in 1893 by a British company, Crompton and Co, but early toasters didn't turn themselves off once the bread was toasted. The first toaster to pop out the toasted bread automatically was invented by Charles Strite in 1919. It went on sale in 1926, just in time for sliced bread.

Born and bread: Nearly everyone in the UK eats bread – 99% of households buy it regularly and more than 12 million loaves of bread are sold every day. We should eat more wholemeal bread, though – 70% of the bread we eat in the UK is white.

Sliced Bread **Form**

Once you have put this **Invention** to good use,
stick your Achieved Star here and fill in the form

Achieved

USE YOUR LOAF

How many different types of bread have you tried? Use the chart below to record the best sandwich you've ever made. Earn your star if you can impress someone with your tasty sandwich invention.

BREAD TYPE

Firstly, choose your favourite type of bread. Tick one of the bread boxes:

White   Brown   Granary   Baguette   Bap   Bagel   Pitta   Ciabatta

How do you like your sandwich?   Traditional   Grilled   Toasted   Oven   Un-buttered   With butter   With margarine

MAIN FILLING

Arguably, the most important part of the sandwich is the filling. Name two essential ingredients in your ultimate savoury sandwich and your sensational sweet sandwich.

SAVOURY

Filling 1

Filling 2

SWEET

Filling 1

Filling 2

EXTRAS

If two fillings aren't enough, then list any extras here that make your creation so special.

Savoury extras

Sweet extras

NAMING

It's no good having the secret to the ultimate sandwich if you don't have a name for it ...

Savoury sandwich name

Sweet sandwich name

Which is your favourite?   Savoury   Sweet

At the same time you can check out these **Things You Wish You'd Invented:**
5: Fast Food • 18: Fizzy Drinks • 20: Thermometer • 27: Pizza
32: Cutlery • 66: Tea • 68: Refrigerator • 77: Banana Suitcase

It needs a little more work, Leonardo ...

Helicopter

Not content with being able to fly – a pretty good trick – someone decided it was vital to be able to hover as well.

Wingless Wonders

The big difference between helicopters and planes is the lack of wings: helicopters use rotors instead. Because of the rotors, helicopters don't need to be moving forward in order to stay up in the air. This means they can do clever things like hover, rotate, fly backwards and stop in mid-air.

The idea of rotors had been around long before the Wright brothers' plane: 1,500 years ago the Chinese had come up with a toy that flew using rotor blades. Leonardo da Vinci's 15th-century notebooks show a drawing of a flying machine that uses rotors (it couldn't really have flown, though).

The Chinese and Leonardo were ahead of their time. It wasn't until the 20th century that helicopters really got off the ground: in 1907 Paul Cornu's helicopter became the first to take off, but it only reached 1.8 m high, it had to be kept stable by men on the ground using sticks, and it managed 20 seconds in the air before it crashed. Various helicopter pioneers worked hard over the next 20 years, improving on the design, making countless test flights. The first helicopter to do much better was designed by German Heinriche Focke and flew in 1936. In 1942 Igor Sikorsky's helicopter became the first to go into production and was used by the US army during the Second World War.

Fasten your seatbelts: Flying a helicopter is very complicated because of the many different ways in which it can move. There's a separate vital control for both hands and both feet and pilots need lots of training and skill. Good concentration is essential.

Helicopter **Form**

Once you have put this **Invention** to good use,
stick your Achieved Star here and fill in the form

Achieved

HELICOPTER

Make your own paper helicopter by following these simple instructions.

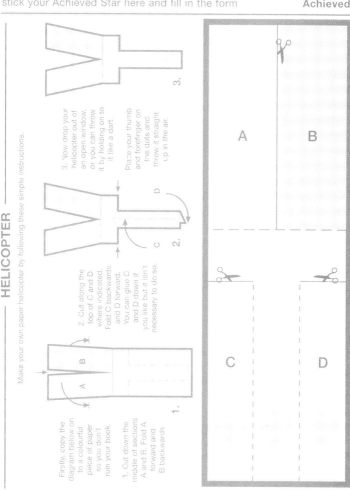

Firstly, copy the diagram below on to a colourful piece of paper so you don't ruin your book.

1. Cut down the middle of sections A and B. Fold A forward and B backwards.

2. Cut along the top of C and D where indicated. Fold C backwards and D forward. You can glue C and D down if you like but it isn't necessary to do so.

3. Now drop your helicopter out of an open window, or you can throw it by holding on to it like a dart.

Place your thumb and forefinger on the dots and throw it straight up in the air.

At the same time you can check out these **Things You Wish You'd Invented:**
13: Satellite • 24: Hot-Air Balloon • 26: Submarine • 31: Compass
47: Radar • 81: Laser • 83: Parachute • 93: Ejector Seat

MON TUE WED THU FRI SAT SUN

Every Day Is Jeans Day

Jeans

However bad your fashion sense, it's hard to go wrong with jeans and a T-shirt. And jeans are comfy and hard-wearing too. Without them, deciding what to wear would be so much more difficult.

Rivet, Rivet

The first jeans, practical cotton trousers for sailors, were made in Genoa, Italy, as long ago as the 1500s. We don't know who first made them, but they were named after the colour they were dyed: in French, *blu de Gêne* (blue of Genoa). Jeans began to be made in serge, a hard-wearing fabric, that came from Nîmes in France, which is how denim got its name: *de Nîmes* (from Nîmes).

In the 1850s, when the USA's gold rush was on, Levi Strauss was in business supplying the mining towns of California with cloth and other dry goods. Jacob Davis was a tailor who had noticed that the jeans he made using Strauss's denim would wear out over time, especially around the pockets. He had the idea of using rivets to make the jeans stronger, and approached Strauss with the idea. Their 'Improvement in Fastening Pocket Openings' received a US patent in 1873 and they used Strauss's money to start their business in making rivetted jeans. Like their 16th-century predecessors, at first rivetted jeans were only worn as work clothes, but by the 1950s they'd become fashionable. In the 1980s designers started making their own brands and jeans became even more popular, as well as more expensive.

The ORIGINAL Levis Strauss: A pair of jeans dating from the 1880s was found in a Nevada mining town in 1998. They were bought by the company that had originally made them, Levi Strauss & Co, for $46,532. That's a lot of cash for old clobber.

Jeans **Form**

Once you have put this **Invention** to good use,
stick your Achieved Star here and fill in the form

Achieved

JEAN GENIE

Jeans are incredibly versatile, which also means they're incredibly popular. If you want to stand out from the crowd, you need to find a way to customise your jeans, making them unique to you. Experiment on an old pair. If they're torn or holey, why not make this a feature, or find some scissors and get creative making shapes, or simply turn them into shorts?

You could use fabric paints or dye to add some colour and create unique designs. You could also attach or sew on extra features. You'll find some ideas to inspire you below. Draw what you did on the outline provided, or stick a photo of your finished product in its place.

ACCESSORISE

Tick the relevant boxes if your
design featured any of the following:

☐ Rips	☐ Cut-out sections
☐ Badges	☐ Sequins
☐ Paper clips	☐ Ribbons
☐ Buttons	☐ Beads
☐ Safety pins	☐ Zips
☐ Different fabrics e.g. lace	

List anything else you
used below

At the same time you can check out these Things You Wish You'd Invented:
19: Birthdays • 37: Fashion • 62: Bling • 75: Teenagers • 94: Flip Flops

Music

Since ancient times, music has been used to help celebrate, tell stories, make protests, and generally cheer everybody up. What would we do without it?

Golden Oldies

Music is common to all cultures all over the world. Far back in human history people must have discovered they could produce interesting sounds with their voices. Someone somewhere must have banged two sticks together to keep time. Of course, no one knows who first came up with a tune, or what it sounded like, because people didn't write anything down in those days.

- The oldest musical instrument ever found is between 43,000 and 82,000 years old. It's part of the thigh bone of a bear with four holes carved into it – it must have been a type of flute.
- The oldest playable musical instrument found so far is 9,000 years old. Several flutes were found in China, made from the wing bones of the red-crowned crane. The best preserved flute has been played and we now know that Stone Age people listened to a sort of weedy recorder.

We don't know what music people played on the Chinese flutes. But we do know what some other ancient music sounded like – the earliest written music that survives today is 3,400 years old and was found on clay tablets in the ancient Syrian city of Ugarit. The ancient Greeks were the first to study music in a scientific way, develop music theory and introduce a system of musical notation.

Deafening silence: 20th-century composer John Cage's *4'33"* is a piece of music in three movements, and was first performed in 1952 on the piano. It is four minutes and thirty-three seconds of complete silence.

Music **Form**

Once you have put this **Invention** to good use,
stick your Achieved Star here and fill in the form

Achieved

MUSIC HALL OF FAME

There are so many music genres, bands and artists that it's impossible to keep up
with them all. Here is a list of bands from each decade from the 1930s to present day.
Can you match the artists to their music?

WE WILL ROCK YOU

ARTIST

| Elvis Presley | Freddie Mercury | Beyoncé Knowles | Michael Jackson |
| Frank Sinatra | John Lennon | Duke Ellington | Kurt Cobain |

BAND   FORMER BAND

| Queen | The Beatles | Nirvana | Destiny's Child |
| The Washingtonians | Tommy Dorsey Orchestra | The Blue Moon Boys | The Jackson Five |

HAD A HIT WITH ...

| 'Smells Like Teen Spirit' | 'Crazy in Love' | 'Don't Get Around Much Anymore' | 'Bohemian Rhapsody' |
| 'She Loves You' | 'My Way' | 'Blue Suede Shoes' | 'Thriller' |

BIG IN THE ...

| 1930s | 1940s | 1950s | 1960s | 1970s | 1980s | 1990s | 2000s |

MUSIC GENRE

| R&B | Pop | Pop/rock | Jazz |
| Grunge | Rock 'n' roll | Glam rock | Swing |

WHERE ARE THEY NOW?

| Died aged 75 from lung cancer | Died aged 82 from a heart attack | Died aged 42 from a heart attack | Died aged 40 after being shot by a fan |
| Died aged 45 from Aids | Career has taken a turn for the worse | Committed suicide aged 27 | Has a successful solo career |

At the same time you can check out these **Things You Wish You'd Invented:**
2: Mobile Phone • 15: Tattoo • 21: Guitar • 25: Poetry • 29: Post-It Notes
35: CDs and DVDs • 75: Teenagers • 81: Laser • 88: Computer • 92: Vinyl Records

Oi! I'm down here!

Radar

Radar is now essential safety equipment for ships and planes, but it was planned as a deadly weapon.

Bouncing Waves

Radar uses radio waves to detect objects and can plot their position, course and speed. Various inventors helped develop it ...

- German physicist Heinrich Hertz discovered radio waves in 1888 and found that they could bounce off other objects.
- In 1904 Christian Hulsmeyer invented a way of detecting ships using radio waves, although his 'telimobiloscope' couldn't measure distance.
- Rudolf Kuhnold demonstrated the first practical radio detection equipment in Germany in 1934.
- In 1935 the British government asked physicist Robert Watson-Watt to research radio waves and their use in destroying enemy planes. Watson-Watt quickly concluded that radio waves couldn't be used as death-ray weapons but discovered that by bouncing radio waves off planes and measuring the delay in the echo, the direction and distance of the plane could be calculated. Only a few weeks after he'd begun his research, Watson-Watt demonstrated radar by plotting the course of an aircraft.
- Radar was developed independently in Germany and the USA and was used extensively in the Second World War to plot enemy ships and planes. A US Navy Commander came up with the name, RAdio Detection And Ranging.

Magnetrons: The radio waves used in radar are generated by magnetrons, invented by John Randall and Henry Boot. Wartime radar operators discovered that magnetrons could be used as water heaters for their tea. Today they are used in microwave ovens.

Radar **Form**

Once you have put this **Invention** to good use,
stick your Achieved Star here and fill in the form

Achieved

THAT SINKING FEELING

See how good your personal radar is by playing battleships, a simple game for two people.

HOW TO PLAY BATTLESHIPS

Cruiser (2 squares) • Destroyer (3 squares) • Destroyer (3 squares) • Battleship (4 squares) • Aircraft carrier (5 squares)

Draw two squares 10 x 10 cm and divide them up into squares, as shown in the example below.
One of these grids will show the position of your fleet; the other is used to locate your opponent's.
Each fleet consists of five ships, including a cruiser (2 squares), two destroyers (3 squares each).
a battleship (4 squares) and an aircraft carrier (5 squares).

YOUR FLEET

THEIR FLEET

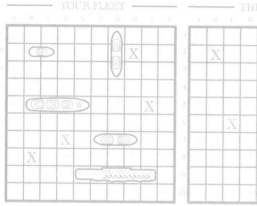

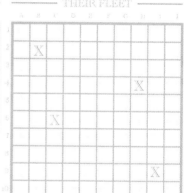

Add your fleet to one of the grids by drawing the shapes of your ships on the squares with a pencil. Place them horizontally and vertically, but not diagonally. See above for an example. Keep your formation hidden from your opponent. Once they have placed their fleet on their own grid, you can start to take pot shots at each other's navy.

Player 1 shouts out a square – for example, 2H. Player 2 shouts out 'HIT' or 'MISS'. Mark your opponent's guesses on **Your Fleet** grid and mark your guesses on **Their Fleet** grid. Each player takes turns even if the other player gets a hit. If a

square with a ship on it is selected, you or your opponent must shout out 'HIT'. If you get a hit, you can now focus on that area until you completely destroy the ship.

Keep taking turns until you manage to sink your opponent's entire fleet (or they sink yours). Play the best of five games and win to earn your star.

How many games did you win? ☐ out of ☐ 5

At the same time you can check out these **Things You Wish You'd Invented:**
2: Mobile Phone • 8: Nuclear Weapons • 13: Satellite
17: Morse Code • 26: Submarine • 44: Helicopter • 90: Maps

Aspirin

You've probably taken aspirin if you've had a headache or a cold. There are other similar drugs available now, but aspirin was the first of its kind.

What a Pain

Aspirin is used to kill pain, reduce swelling and thin the blood to help heart-attack and stroke patients. It's related to a natural remedy that's been known for thousands of years.

- About 2,500 years ago, the ancient Greek doctor Hippocrates wrote about the healing properties of a tea made from the bark of a willow tree. It's also mentioned as a remedy in writing from other ancient civilisations in the Middle East and North America.
- In 1763 an English Reverend, Edmund Stone, described how farm workers used willow bark to make a cure for fevers.
- In 1838 the Italian chemist Rafaele Piria discovered a way to extract the active ingredient of willow bark – salicin – and convert it into salicylic acid. But, used on its own, salicylic acid gives patients stomach pains and sickness.
- In 1899 Felix Hoffman, an employee of the pharmaceutical company Bayer, used his arthritic father as a guinea pig. After trying various compounds, he discovered that acetylsalicylic acid was effective and free from side effects. It was a great discovery, and a great relief for Hoffman's father.
- Acetylsalicylic acid, called aspirin, went on sale as a powder. It was an instant success.

A few days after he'd invented aspirin, Hoffman invented another drug, heroin, which was marketed at the same time. At first, heroin was more successful because people believed it to be healthier ... then they discovered that it was also addictive.

Aspirin **Form**

Once you have put this **Invention** to good use,
stick your Achieved Star here and fill in the form

Achieved

——— WHAT IS IT GOOD FOR? ———

Everyone knows that eating certain foods can help you stay fit and healthy, especially food rich in vitamins and minerals. Before pharmaceutical drugs were available, though, people had to rely far more on different types of food to not only keep them well, but help them feel better when they did get ill.

——— A QUICK FIX ———

Take a look at the list below: can you match the food with the ailment it treats?

1. SAGE	a. DIGESTION	e. HOT FLUSHES, SORE THROATS, SWEATING
2. LAVENDER	b. TRAVEL SICKNESS, FLATULENCE, INDIGESTION	
3. GINGER		f. COLDS AND FLU, MINOR INFECTIONS, WOUND HEALING, ACNE, ALLERGIES
4. PEPPERMINT	c. INSOMNIA	
5. THYME	d. COUGHS, CHEST CONGESTION	
6. ECHINACEA		g. IRRITABLE BOWEL SYNDROME
7. DANDELION		

——— CURE ALL ———

Choose some healthy foods and herbs and see if you can create the ultimate cure-all smoothie. Try different combinations to find one you like. Most will probably taste disgusting, but no pain, no gain!

GOOD SMOOTHIE! **BAD SMOOTHIE!**

List the good ingredients you used

List the bad ingredients you used

Did it make you feel better?

Did it make you feel better?

On a scale of 1–5, how good did it taste?

I rate it [ ] out of 5

I rate it [ ] out of 5

Will you make it again?

Will you make it again?

——— HIT THE JACKPOT! ———

Try this food trivia quiz. Which of the following ...

1. ... has the most vitamin C?

ORANGE BROCCOLI LEMON

2. ... is 92% water?

TOMATO LEMON WATERMELON

3. ... causes 300 accidents a year in the UK?

WATERMELON BANANA PEANUT

4. ... is the world's most popular fruit?

BANANA ORANGE TOMATO

5. ... was known as 'mad apple' in Italy?

AUBERGINE PEPPER BROCCOLI

6. ... can be used in the production of dynamite?

PEPPER AUBERGINE PEANUT

 At the same time you can check out these **Things You Wish You'd Invented**:
63: Anaesthetics • 72: X-ray • 79: Toothpaste • 84: Anti-Ageing Pills
91: Antibiotics • 95: Soap • 97: Alcoholic Drinks

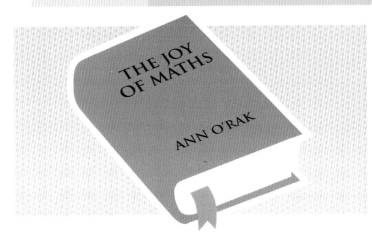

Homework Machine

If getting up early every day to go to school and having to stay there for *hours* is cruel, then bringing a bit of school home with you at the end of the day is just prolonging the torture! Unfortunately, homework is something we all have to suffer. Until someone comes up with this brilliant invention …

Whistle While We Homework

If such a machine did exist, then all that time normally lost to homework could be reclaimed. No longer would you have to endure the last-minute homework rush on Sunday nights, or valuable TV time being held to ransom by parents who insist that homework comes first. But how would it work?

* You could invent a duplication machine (**Invention** No. 55) and create a second 'you' to do the work. Although you might have a strike on your hands when the other 'you' realised the fun he/she was missing out on.
* You could go for the more traditional method, and bribe a friend or sibling to do the work for you. (Warning: this could be rather expensive.)
* Some teachers and politcans believe that a type of homework machine already exists: the internet. But even the internet can't do everything you want it to, and it certainly can't imitate your handwriting.

The main problem with the methods above is that you wouldn't actually learn anything, which would become a problem in lessons and exams. A really clever machine would incorporate a Know-It-All Hat (**Invention** No. 96), so that your brain wouldn't miss out on the learning, just the hard work!

Web of deceit: The internet may be able to help you with your homework, but don't rely on it too much. It is reported that only 90% of the information on the web is true, so you should always double-check your facts. Stick to websites designed for schools to be on the safe side.

Homework Machine **Form**

Once you have put this **Invention** to good use,
stick your Achieved Star here and fill in the form

Achieved

-- HOMEWORK --

If you add up all the hours you put into doing your homework, by the time you leave school you will
have clocked up months! Now it's your turn to set the homework. Write a quiz for your teacher to
do. Ask them the questions you think EVERYONE should know the answers to, and when they've
completed it, grade them and set them another one for next week!

Teacher's Test

GRADE

What comment would you add? Delete as appropriate

Excellent / Good effort / You can do better
Must try harder / See me after school

At the same time you can check out these **Things You Wish You'd Invented:**
4: Cloning • 16: Pencils • 29: Post-It Notes • 30: Magic • 42: School • 50: Printing
75: Teenagers • 76: Intelligent Robots • 100: Chindogu • 101: Room 101

Printing

If it wasn't for printing, a scribe would have to copy out this entire book word for word. There wouldn't be many copies and they'd cost a bomb.

Making an Impression

One of the earliest surviving printed books is a Buddhist text, written in Chinese and dating back to AD 848. It was printed using wooden blocks which had the words and illustrations carved into them. In the 11th century the Chinese invented a new way of printing, using moveable raised letters made, firstly, from clay, but later wood and then metal. These letters could be moved into place, inked, then stamped on to paper – as many copies as were needed. The only time-consuming bit was putting the letters and words in the right order in the first place.

But the printing invention that really changed the world was the printing press, invented by Johannes Gutenberg in Germany in 1440. It wasn't based on the Chinese invention but on olive- and wine-presses and it was so good that for more than 300 years hardly any changes were needed. More efficient versions were made after the industrial revolution, but still they used the same basic design.

The printing press created a revolution: for the first time, ideas and information could be easily communicated to lots of people much more cheaply than ever before. More people learned to read as a result.

Stop the press! The printing press led to the development of different kinds of printed material: the first newspaper was published in Germany in 1605; the first magazine appeared in London in 1731. It was called *The Gentleman's Magazine* and it ran for over 170 years.

Printing **Form**

Once you have put this **Invention** to good use,
stick your Achieved Star here and fill in the form

Achieved

I SAY POTATO, YOU SAY POT-ART-O

It may be primitive, but it's fun too. Get a potato and start
printing within minutes, using your own simple or grand designs.

WHAT YOU NEED

a potato, a pencil, a knife, paint or ink, paper

WHAT TO DO

Choose a big, dry, raw spud,
the bigger the better.

Chop it in half.

Draw your design on the cut
end of your spud-half in pencil.

Using a knife,
score around
the outline of
your design ...

... and then cut away the
bits you don't want to print.
You're ready to go.

DESIGN IDEAS

Here are some ideas to get the potato rolling.
Start with an easy one, and work your way up
to the more complex designs.

Your initials   **ABC**

Some of your
favourite things

Your
profile

A wallpaper pattern   A potato planet

YOUR RESULTS

Record your most successful potato print design here

At the same time you can check out these Things You Wish You'd Invented:
5: Fast Food • 6: Photography • 15: Tattoo • 16: Pencils • 25: Poetry
29: Post-It Notes • 46: Music • 52: Language • 71: Numbers • 87: Passport • 90: Maps

Make-up

Make-up is supposed to make us look more beautiful. From the earliest times people have used it in an attempt to increase their pulling power.

Drop Dead Gorgeous

- The earliest evidence of make-up was found in ancient Egyptian tombs dating from around 5,000 years ago. Both men and women used skin cream, perfumes, eye shadow, eyeliner, mascara, lip colour and rouge.
- The ancient Chinese, Greeks and Romans also used all kinds of make-up. A 1,800-year-old ancient Roman skin cream was discovered recently in London, the oldest preserved cosmetic ever found.
- Poisons, especially lead, were used in ancient cosmetics and continued to be used until the 1800s. Eyeshadows, lipsticks and face powder all contained dangerous chemicals, and women made their eyes sparkle with deadly nightshade. Skin was whitened with powder containing lead because pale-skinned women were supposed to be beautiful.
- Ironically, from the 1920s darker skin became more desirable – so some women started to use make-up or dye to make their skins look tanned.
- Victorian and Edwardian ladies tried to keep their beauty secrets secret, because, for a period, make-up was frowned upon and associated only with actresses and prostitutes. Rich ladies would sneak into beauty parlours by the back door.
- By the 20th century make-up became acceptable again, and today the cosmetics industry is worth billions of pounds.

 Looks fishy ... 'Pearl essence' is a lipstick ingredient that gives a shimmery effect. It sounds rather lovely but in fact it's fish scales – mostly herring. And cerebrosides, found in moisturising skin-care products, are animal brain cells or nervous system tissue.

Make-up **Form**

Once you have put this **Invention** to good use,
stick your Achieved Star here and fill in the form

Achieved

GRUESOME MAKE-UP TIPS

Make-up doesn't have to be used for beautification. Here are some examples of face make-up
you can use to scare your family with! WARNING: Before you put the paint all over your face,
test a small patch on the back of your hand, as your skin may be sensitive to certain face paints.
The main colours you'll need are black, white, green, grey, red and brown.

VAMPIRE — FRANKENSTEIN'S MONSTER — DEVIL

A simple transformation: use white
paint all over your face, except
around your eyes. You can fill in the
eye area with red, black or grey.
Finally, paint two triangles on your
bottom lip for fangs.

Paint your whole face green
and darken under your brow and in
your eye sockets with brown paint.
Make two bolts from chunky
plastic bottle tops and fasten them
around your neck with elastic.

Paint your whole face red,
darkening the area around your
eyes with black or brown. Then add
a moustache, beard and wicked
eyebrows. Make two horns from
card and fasten them on your head.

ZOMBIE — WEREWOLF — SKELETON

Paint your whole face grey and
darken the areas around
your eyes. Then draw thin black
lines up from your mouth to make
you look old and haggard. Finally,
paint a red drip from your mouth
like blood. You could also add
some brown scars to your face.

You need two different shades
of brown for this monster. Cover
your face in the lighter brown
and then draw thick hair as
shown with the darker brown.
Don't forget to add white fangs on
your lips and a black wolfy nose.

Paint the white areas of the
skull face first as shown, and
then use black paint in the
non-bone areas for definition.
Remember to paint eye holes,
a triangular shape for the
missing nose and teeth on
your top and bottom lips.

 At the same time you can check out these **Things You Wish You'd Invented:**
19: Birthdays • 37: Fashion • 39: Toilets and Toilet Paper
62: Bling • 75: Teenagers • 85: Mirror

Language

Thank goodness for language: without it we'd be trying to communicate using grunts and hand signals, which are quite difficult to write down ...

In the Beginning Was the Word

No one knows when people – or our prehistoric ancestors – first used language. It's possible that the human-like creatures that existed 1.5 million years ago had already developed some kind of verbal communication, because the main areas of the brain associated with speech had evolved by then. But most experts think that language probably developed round about 50–60,000 years ago, because that's when lots of different innovations, like painting, sculpture and complex social organisation, appeared in human society.

It's not surprising that we don't know *how* exactly language came about, either – no one wrote anything down that might tell us. Perhaps hand gestures were used before speech, then words gradually developed from noises made to accompany them. Or perhaps language evolved from cries to warn others of danger.

However it happened, language soon acquired a wide vocabulary and complicated grammar, which we need to express all the clever thoughts we have. It was only about five thousand years ago that people started writing things down and not long after that someone invented spelling tests!

Squawk talk: No other animals have developed language, but a chimpanzee called Washoe was the first animal to be taught sign language. Alex, an African grey parrot at Brandeis University in Massachusetts, speaks and seems to understand language, and can count up to six.

Language **Form**

Once you have put this **Invention** to good use,
stick your Achieved Star here and fill in the form

Achieved

PIG LATIN

Pig Latin (also known as 'backslang') is a word game that can also be used as a secret code,
so your snooping parents can't listen in on your private conversations.

Variations on backslang were used by criminals in Victorian London to talk to each other
without their plans being rumbled. English butchers and grocers are also known to have
spoken a type of backslang. Nowadays it is only really used as a bit of fun.

RULES

The rules for Pig Latin are very
simple. This is how it works:

1. With words that begin with a
consonant, take the first letter and
place it at the back of the word then add
'ay'. For example 'cat' would become
'atcay'. Here are a few more examples:

school = choolsay
holiday = olidayhay
Pig Latin = igpay atinlay

2. This rule also applies to words with
silent letters at the start, such as ...

know = nowkay
honest = onesthay
gnome = nomegay

3. With words that begin with vowels
you only add 'ay' (or, if you prefer, yay).
For example:

out = outay
apple = appleay
offer = offeray

That's pretty much it!
So the sentence 'Meet me at midnight'
becomes 'Eetmay emay atay idnightmay'

Ready? Now you try it!

Find a friend and learn to speak
and write Pig Latin together.

Your name (in Pig Latin)

The name of your Pig Latin pal

Did you find learning
Pig Latin difficult?   y/n

Did you find understanding
Pig Latin difficult?   y/n

Who was the best at speaking Pig Latin?

What is your favourite phrase in Pig Latin?

Have you used Pig Latin code to talk   y/n
privately in public?

If yes, where?

At the same time you can check out these **Things You Wish You'd Invented**:
2: Mobile Phone • 17: Morse Code • 25: Poetry • 38: Sign Language
42: School • 50: Printing • 78: Language Decoder

Yo-yo

The yo-yo is thought to be one of the oldest toys in the world – they've been around and up and down for roughly 2,500 years.

Round, Round, Get Around ...

- The world's first yo-yo was invented in ancient Greece round about 500–400 BC. We don't know exactly who worked out that two discs (made from metal, clay or wood), an axle and a piece of string could be so much fun.
- The word 'yo-yo' isn't ancient Greek but probably comes from the Philippines, where yo-yoing was popular for centuries.
- In the late 1700s the yo-yo finally arrived in Europe. They were known as bandalores or quizzes in England, and also 'the Prince of Wales's toy', and became fashionable with posh people.
- By the 19th century Americans were playing with yo-yos.
- In the 1920s Pedro Flores, originally from the Philippines, began to make and sell yo-yos in California. A businessman called Donald Duncan bought the yo-yo company, trademarked the name and advertised the toy. He also made some improvements to the design, making yo-yo tricks easier to do.
- The yo-yos became so popular that Duncan's factory produced 3,600 yo-yos an hour in the 1930s.
- The toy has gone in and out of fashion since then and various improvements have led to new and ever more flashy tricks. Every year the World Yo-yo Contest takes place, drawing competitors from all over the globe to perform in eight different categories.

Space, 1985: Yo-yos were taken on board the space shuttle *Discovery*, as part of the Toys in Space project, to observe the effects of zero gravity on yo-yoing. In 1992 the space shuttle *Atlantis* also had yo-yos on board, in order to film a video of slow-motion yo-yoing!

Yo-yo **Form**

Once you have put this **Invention** to good use,
stick your Achieved Star here and fill in the form

Achieved

——— YO-YO TRICKS ———

Try these moves to get you started. For more tricks, go to: **www.yoyoing/beginner**

——— GRAVITY PULL ———

1. Start position

2. Release

☐ Completed

Snap back up

3.

——— FORWARD PASS ———

Start with your hand by your side, then bring it forward, releasing the yo-yo at the same time. Catch the yo-yo in your hand.

Start position

1.

2.

☐ Completed

3.

——— AROUND THE WORLD ———

1.

Start with your hand by your side. Pull your hand forward and flick the yo-yo away (1). When the yo-yo is at its furthest point (2), make it go through a 360 loop as many times as you can (3). Then catch it (4).

2.

3.

4.

☐ Completed

——— SLEEPER ———

Start position

3. Hold for as long as possible

4.

2. Release the yo-yo, letting it extend fully

Snap back up

☐ Completed

——— WALKING THE DOG ———

1.

Start position

2.

3.

4.

5.

Flick the yo-yo down to the floor, slightly behind you (2). When the yo-yo is on the floor, walk forwards (3). The yo-yo should 'walk' past you (4). Flick your wrist to retrieve the yo-yo (5).

☐ Completed

 At the same time you can check out these **Things You Wish You'd Invented**:
14: **Playing Cards** • 19: **Birthdays** • 23: **Plastic** • 41: **Football**
82: **Skateboard** • 96: **Know-It-All Hat** • 100: **Chindogu**

Steam Engine

No one uses the power of steam much today, but steam once drove trains, ships, factories and the entire industrial revolution.

Letting Off Steam

It might surprise you to hear that an ancient Greek called Hero invented the steam engine in about AD 50. The ancient Greeks weren't especially impressed with it, though, and couldn't really see its potential for moving things about. So they forgot about it.

It was another 1,650 years before Thomas Savery came up with another steam engine – a steam pump, for pumping water out of mines. Unfortunately it had a tendency to blow up. In 1712 Thomas Newcomen built a better one that didn't explode so often, but it was still pretty inefficient. Over the 1760s and 70s Scottish inventor James Watt improved on these earlier versions, and his one was so good that he's become famous for it. But Watt's were still mainly used for pumping water.

In 1804 Richard Trevithick tested out a steam engine that moved, but he didn't have much success with it. George Stephenson was the inventor of the first really good moving steam engine. Initially these locomotives were used for hauling heavy goods from mines and quarries. In 1829 his steam engine, *Rocket*, won a competition run by the Liverpool and Manchester Railway to find a locomotive that could carry goods and passengers. *Rocket* could pull a coach full of passengers at 39 km/h – and there were no cancellations!

Train victim no. 1: George Stephenson's *Rocket* was responsible for the first train fatality. It ran over and killed MP William Huskisson at the opening of the Liverpool and Manchester Railway in 1830 as the MP made to cross the track to speak to the prime minister.

Steam Engine **Form**

Once you have put this **Invention** to good use,
stick your Achieved Star here and fill in the form

Achieved

--- **OLD TRAINS VS NEW TRAINS** ---

Trains have moved on a lot in the last 180 years. A French TGV train became the fastest train on
tracks in April 2007, reaching a speed of 356 mph (574.8 km/h). Going really fast has its
advantages, and it can be exhilarating, but there is an undeniable charm about steam trains,
which is why there are still a number of steam train services running around the UK. Take a trip on
a old steam train and a modern train and record your experiences below. How did they differ?

Type of steam train	Type of modern train

Number of steam train	Number of modern train

If the train had a name, write it below

If the train had a name, write it below

Where did your journey start and end?

Where did your journey start and end?

| | to | |

| | to | |

Give marks out of five for the following:

Give marks out of five for the following:

Speed /5   Comfort /5

Speed /5   Comfort /5

Punctuality /5   Scenery /5

Punctuality /5   Scenery /5

Rate your steam train experience overall

☆ ☆ ☆ ☆ ☆
Awful OK Good Great Excellent

Rate your modern train experience overall

☆ ☆ ☆ ☆ ☆
Awful OK Good Great Excellent

--- **CONCLUSION** ---

Which train did you prefer and why?

At the same time you can check out these **Things You Wish You'd Invented:**
12: Dynamite • 20: Thermometer • 24: Hot-Air Balloon
26: Submarine • 33: Battery • 58: Roller Coaster

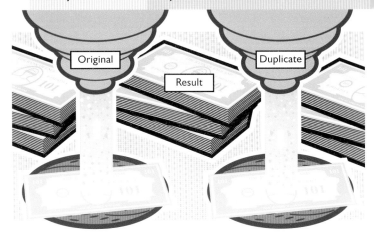

Duplication Machine

Life would never be the same again with a fully functioning duplication machine! You'd never run out of money or be down to your last Rolo. And think of the good you could do ... you'd be able to save animals on the brink of extinction! And if you could copy yourself, the real you could have endless fun while the other did all your schooling and homework (**Invention** No. 49 Should you ever be tempted to copy yourself, however, you should take the precautions below. Your duplicate would need to know who's boss.

Two's Company, Three's a Crowd

- Make sure that you're in charge of delegating the workload. If you don't la down the law from the start, your duplicate could take over. It might be YOU who ends up doing all the work while your duplicate has all the fun.
- Build a security system into the machine and change the password as soor as you've duplicated yourself. If your duplicate were able to use the machine and copy themselves over and over, you'd quickly be overthrown by your duplicates and almighty chaos would ensue!
- Make two T-shirts to be worn at all times – one for you, saying 'Original', and the other for your duplicate, saying 'Copy' – so no one gets confused.

As you can see, duplication could be fraught with danger. And remember tha if you could copy anything any number of times, that thing would quickly los its value, and nothing and nobody would be unique any more. It sounds grea in theory, but think twice before inventing this machine!

Fool's gold: The highest value US banknote ever minted was for $100,000, but this didn't stop ambitious counterfeiter, Tekle Zigetta, who was caught forging $1 billion-dollar bills in 2006. Now the US government has stopped the production of dollar bills above $100 in value.

Duplication Machine **Form**

Once you have put this **Invention** to good use,
stick your Achieved Star here and fill in the form

Achieved

CARBON COPY

Take a look at the three COPY-CAT challenges below.
Firstly, the quickest way to annoy someone is to copy EVERYTHING that person does. Choose your
victim. Repeat everything they say out loud and copy every move they make. It'll drive them crazy!

Write the name of victim 1 below | Write the name of victim 2 below | Write the name of victim 3 below

| How long did it take to annoy them? | mins | secs | How long did it take to annoy them? | mins | secs | How long did it take to annoy them? | mins | secs |

BE YOUR BEST

Become your best friend! See if you can do an impressive impression of them. If your best
friend is your twin, you've got a head start! See if you can pick up their characteristics and
favourite sayings without being too mean! Assess your efforts using the star ratings below.

Who did you impersonate?

How much did you sound like them?
☆ 1 ☆ 2 ☆ 3 ☆ 4 ☆ 5

How much did you look like them?
☆ 1 ☆ 2 ☆ 3 ☆ 4 ☆ 5

How well did you act like them?
☆ 1 ☆ 2 ☆ 3 ☆ 4 ☆ 5

Phone up a mutual friend and try to
fool them into thinking you are your
best friend. Did you succeed?   y/n

How did your best friend feel about
your impression?

ROLE REVERSE

Finally, see if your best friend can do a decent impression of you!

Who impersonated you?

Now give your friend star ratings ...
How much did they sound like you?
☆ 1 ☆ 2 ☆ 3 ☆ 4 ☆ 5

How much did they look like you?
☆ 1 ☆ 2 ☆ 3 ☆ 4 ☆ 5

How well did they act like you?
☆ 1 ☆ 2 ☆ 3 ☆ 4 ☆ 5

Did you learn anything about your own
behaviour from this experiment?   y/n

If yes, what did you learn?

At the same time you can check out these **Things You Wish You'd Invented:**
4: Cloning • 9: Money • 30: Magic • 49: Homework Machine • 98: Terraforming

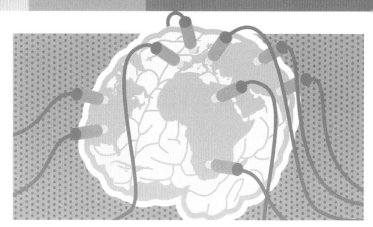

World Wide Web

Where would we be without access to all that astonishing information, email and messaging, shopping, blogs, home videos and bad jokes?

Tangled Web

There would be no web without the internet. Before its invention, you could only connect to one other computer at a time, using an expensive telephone connection. The internet began as a computer network in the US defence department, which was designed to let computers communicate with one another even if there were a nuclear war. Thankfully, Armageddon never arrived, but the internet did. It was made possible by 'packet switching', a way of sending data invented in the 1960s by Donald Davies and Paul Baran, working independently of one another in the UK and the USA.

Most people's experience of the internet is the World Wide Web – all those billions of pages of incredibly useful, or sometimes completely useless, stuff. That was invented by an English computer scientist called Tim Berners-Lee who was working for the European Centre for Nuclear Research (CERN) in Switzerland. His invention meant that the information on the internet was much easier to get at, and made it possible to easily transfer text, images, sound and video. The web was being used by the scientists at CERN in 1990, and the following year it was available for everyone. Today there are more than 1 billion users around the world.

info.cern.ch: This is the address of the first ever website, created in 1990. The indexed World Wide Web now contains over 14 billion pages – and that's just the indexable pages (the ones everybody can find on search engines). And there are new ones added every day.

World Wide Web **Form**

Once you have put this **Invention** to good use,
stick your Achieved Star here and fill in the form

Achieved

CORRECT ROUTER

The diagram below isn't just a fun puzzle – it also roughly demonstrates how your computer sends and receives information via the internet. Once requested, the information travels through a series of connections, including modems, ISP (Internet Service Providers) ports and routers. On the diagram below these are collectively represented by '■'.

Routers help to get your messages from one computer to another. There is not one set route to send information – it depends on which will be quickest. The combinations are limitless, but you still end up with the same information. Now look at the puzzle below. Find the correct route from your computer to the 101 Things website.

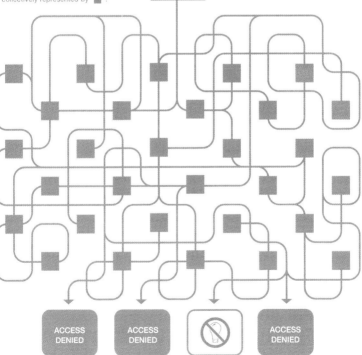

ACCESS DENIED

ACCESS DENIED

ACCESS DENIED

www.101thingstodo.co.uk

At the same time you can check out these Things You Wish You'd Invented:
2: Mobile Phone • 6: Photography • 7: Time Zones • 13: Satellite • 14: Playing Cards
19: Birthdays • 25: Poetry • 35: CDs and DVDs • 75: Teenagers • 88: Computer

Concrete

Concrete is a mixture of cement*, gravel or sand, and water. It's used more than any other man-made material – yes, even more than plastic.

Rock Hard

People knew about concrete thousands of years ago ...

- The ancient Mesopotamians, Assyrians, Chinese and Egyptians all used types of concrete. The oldest concrete ever found was used to make the floors of Stone-Age homes built near the River Danube over 7,000 years ago.
- The ancient Romans used a type of concrete quite similar to the kind we use today. They discovered that adding volcanic ash made it set under water, and adding horse hair made it less likely to shrink.
- Everyone forgot about concrete for a few centuries. Eventually, French architect Philibert de l'Orme wrote about the ingredients of the concrete he used in the 16th century.
- In the 18th century, engineer John Smeaton invented a hard concrete using quicklime. He also came up with a new concrete that hardened under water, and used it to rebuild Eddystone Lighthouse in Cornwall in 1793.
- Today extremely strong concrete can be made by reinforcing it with steel. It's even possible to make concrete that conducts electricity and concrete that transmits light.

Concrete production has high energy costs that make it very bad for the environment. But the use of recycled material is becoming more common.

---

*Cement is a substance used to bind other materials, because when mixed with water it sets and hardens. Concrete, mortar and grout use cement, which is usually made from a calcium source, like limestone, and a silicone source, like clay.

Concrete **Form**

Once you have put this **Invention** to good use,
stick your Achieved Star here and fill in the form

Achieved

CON-CREATIONS

There are some incredible buildings and monuments around the world, built for a
variety of reasons and out of a variety of materials. Can you match each building below
to the amazing facts about them? Award yourself bonus points if you can guess which
five out of the eight buildings used concrete in their construction.

BUILD AND CONSTRUCT

BUILDING

| Empire State Building | Christ the Redeemer | Eiffel Tower | The Tower |
| Opera House | The Great Wall | The Colosseum | Petra |

LOCATION

| Rio de Janeiro, Brazil | Sydney, Australia | China | New York City, USA |
| Jordan | Paris, France | London, UK | Rome, Italy |

FUNCTION

| Gladiator arena | To keep invaders out | Music venue | A city of tombs and temples |
| Offices | Prison | Radio broadcasting tower | Statue |

DOB (DATE OF BUILD)

| 93c-AD 70 | 221 BC ONWARDS | AD 70-82 ONWARDS | AD 1078 ONWARDS |
| 1887-1889 | 1926-1931 | 1930-1931 | 1957-1973 |

DESIGNED OR COMMISSIONED BY ...

| William the Conqueror | Emperor Vespasian | Shreve, Lamb and Harmon Associates | Heitor da Silva Costa |
| Gustave Eiffel | Unknown | Qin Shi Huang | Jørn Utzon |

THAT'S AMAZING!

The entire site is carved out of rock inside a canyon.

Known as the world's longest graveyard, due to the number of dead workers buried alongside it

It was only supposed to stand for 20 years and was considered an eyesore by many

Could be entirely flooded so mock sea battles could be staged

The building design is based on the segments of an orange

It weighs 700 tonnes and stands 700 m above sea level

Believed to be the most haunted place in the UK

The spire at the top was originally designed as an airship mooring

---

At the same time you can check out these **Things You Wish You'd Invented**:
8: Nuclear Weapons • 10: Time Machine • 59: Glass • 98: Terraforming

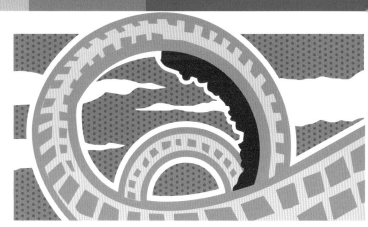

Roller Coaster

If your favourite entertainment is plunging down a 97-degree incline at over 200 km/h, you'd probably like to thank the inventor of the roller coaster.

Thrills and Spills

People managed to find ways of terrifying themselves at high speeds long before roller coasters. In the 1700s the Russians built steep icy hills that people slid down on seats made of wood or ice. Later, wheels were attached. They didn't have many safety features. Modern-day roller coasters began in the USA ...

- A steep 14-km switchback railway track used for delivering coal in Pennsylvania was built in 1827. People paid 50 cents each to ride on it.
- La Marcus Adna Thompson created a 'Switchback Railway' in 1884 as an amusement ride. It wasn't wildly exciting but it was the first roller coaster.
- Rides soon became popular and new and better roller coasters were built, including the first one that formed a circuit, built by Charles Alcoke.
- One of the first roller coasters to loop the loop was the Flip Flap, opened in Brooklyn in 1895. It was extremely dangerous so it was soon dismantled
- Wooden roller coasters appeared all over the world in the early 20th century. By 1959 the first steel track was used in Disneyland's Matterhorn Bobslides and 80 years after the disastrous Flip Flap, the Corkscrew safely looped the loop at Knott's Berry Farm, California.
- Kingda Ka in New Jersey, opened in 2005, is the world's fastest roller coaster at 206 km/h and has the longest drop: 127 m.

The oldest roller coaster that still works is Leap the Dips at Lakemont Park, Pennsylvania. It first opened in 1902. In some languages, the word for 'roller coaster' translates as 'Russian mountain', remembering the invention's ice-slide origins.

Roller Coaster **Form**

Once you have put this **Invention** to good use,
stick your Achieved Star here and fill in the form

Achieved

--- **PARK AND RIDE** ---

They may turn your stomach inside out and put your heart in your mouth, but whichever way you
look at it, whether it be upside down, sideways or loop the loop, roller coasters are ace.

--- **THE PARK** ---

Name your favourite amusement/theme park

Where is the amusement/theme park?

I have ridden [0,0,0] per cent of the rides in the park

How many times have you visited your favourite amusement park? [0,0] times

--- **THE RIDE** ---

Name your favourite roller coaster

What's the longest you've had to queue to get on it? [0,0] hours [0,0] mins

How many of the following does your favourite roller coaster have?

Rolls [0] Climbs [0] Drops [0] Loops [0] Tunnels [0]

How many times have you ridden it? [0,0,0] times

How long does the ride last in seconds? [0,0,0] secs

Find out how fast it goes ... [0,0,0] mph

... and what g (gravity) force the ride reaches [0.0] G's

--- **THE CONSEQUENCES** ---

On a roller coaster, have you ever ...

Screamed? Laughed? Cried? Thrown up? Passed out?

[ ] [ ] [ ] [ ] [ ]

Have any of the above put you off going on a roller coaster again? [y/n]

--- **THE REST** ---

The scariest ride you've ever been on

The most boring ride you've ever been on

The ride that made you feel most sick

At the same time you can check out these **Things You Wish You'd Invented:**
5: Fast Food • 19: Birthdays • 46: Music • 54: Steam Engine • 75: Teenagers

LET THERE
BE LIGHT!

Glass

Glass is useful for all sorts of things, especially windows. Before glass, homes must either have been very dark but warm, or light but cold.

Smashing Stuff

Glass is sand that's been heated to a very high temperature. Obsidian is a natural glass, made by volcanic eruptions millions of years ago. Lightning strikes on sand also produce natural glass, called fulgarites.

We don't know when, where or how the first synthetic glass was made, or who invented it. Someone probably invented it by accident. As far as we know, the ancient Egyptians and Mesopotamians were the first to use it, as glass beads for jewellery, around 2500 BC. A thousand years later, the Egyptians were making glass bottles in moulds.

Around 10 BC, someone in Syria realised that glass could be blown: if you put a blob of liquid glass on the end of a hollow tube and blow, you can make it into a bubble, then shape it to produce bottles, glasses, bowls and other objects. (This takes a bit of practice, obviously.)

The first glass window panes were made in the Middle Ages. The most common method was to blow liquid glass into a disc, which could then be cut and flattened into panes. Windows were made in this way until the 1800s, when a method of making glass in plates was invented. Soon ordinary people were able to look out of the window and keep out the rain at the same time.

 People in glass houses shouldn't throw stones ... Early window glass was quite difficult to see through. Until the late 1700s, anything seen through a glass window wasn't admissible as evidence in an English law court.

Glass **Form**

Once you have put this **Invention** to good use,
stick your Achieved Star here and fill in the form

Achieved

A TOUCH OF GLASS

Make your own stained-glass window and give these medieval church builders a run for their money! The way stained glass is made hasn't really changed since the Middle Ages – until someone invented coloured tissue paper, that is.

WHAT YOU NEED

tissue paper in various colours, a thick black marker, black card,
glue, a pencil, white card, a white coloured pencil, scissors

WHAT TO DO

1. Draw your stained-glass design on a piece of white card. When it's finished, go over the lines of the drawing with a thick black marker pen.

2. Carefully cut out your design, then place this template over a piece of black card and trace around the cut-out with a white pencil. Remove the template to find your design traced on to the black card.

3. Now you need to cut out your design on the black card very carefully. This is the frame. You can use your original white card template again to trace the tissue paper shapes.

4. Make sure when you cut out the tissue paper that you make all the shapes a bit bigger than you have drawn them, so there is room to glue them to the frame.

5. Glue the tissue-paper shapes into place behind the gaps in your design. Once you have finished, stick it to a window and watch the sunlight stream through it.

 At the same time you can check out these **Things You Wish You'd Invented**:
6: Photography • 11: Fingerprinting • 15: Tattoo
40: Spectacles • 61: Microscope and Telescope • 62: Bling

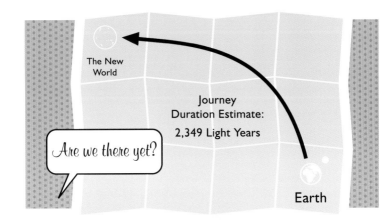

Inter-Stellar Travel

The universe is really very big indeed. So it seems a shame that we're confined to just one tiny little bit of it.

Warp Drive

At the moment, no one knows whether travel to other star systems is ever going to be possible. If you want to invent something really cool, here are just two of the problems you'll have to overcome.

Speed: A light year is the distance travelled by light in one year. Apart from the Sun, a mere 150 million km away, our nearest star is Proxima Centauri, which is 4.2 light years away. Current space rockets can't reach anywhere near the speed of light. It would take the *Voyager* spacecraft, which can travel at 60,000 km/h, 80,000 years to get to Proxima Centauri! You'll have to work out a way of achieving speeds close to or exceeding the speed of light (about 1,000,000,000 km/h). Do some research on worm holes, warp drives and space drives.

Fuel: If *Voyager* were to try and set off on its 80,000-year journey, it would need more fuel than we could ever find. Even nuclear rockets would need to take thousands of supertankers of fuel with them. So you'll have to find a new way of converting energy into motion without using fuel. Tricky.

Even though the cleverest scientists in the world are applying their mighty brains to these problems, it doesn't look as though we'll be travelling to distant stars any time soon. But don't let that put you off – get inventing.

Big numbers: Galaxies up to 16 billion light years away can be seen from Earth with the most powerful telescopes. There are more than 100 billion galaxies in the Universe. It makes you think there must be life out there somewhere, doesn't it?

Inter-Stellar Travel **Form**

Once you have put this **Invention** to good use,
stick your Achieved Star here and fill in the form

Achieved

A PLACE IN SPACE

Only four robotic spacecraft have earned the title of 'inter-stellar probes': *Pioneer 10*, *Pioneer 11*, *Voyager 1* and *Voyager 2*. Of the four, *Voyager 1* (launched on 5 September 1977) has travelled the furthest distance. Its original mission was to take a close-up look at Jupiter and Saturn and transmit its data back to Earth. After completing this mission successfully, *Voyager 1* was given a new mission: to boldly go where no probe has gone before: out of our solar system. Even after 30 years of operations, *Voyager 1* is still sending back its data and it is hoped that it will keep on communicating for many years to come. *Voyager 1* is now over 10 billion miles from the Sun and travels at around a million miles a day! By 2017 it is believed that *Voyager 1* will leave the heliosphere (the edge of space that is influenced by our Sun).

A JOURNEY TO FAR, FAR AWAY

The diagram below shows *Voyager 1*'s journey so far. *Voyager 1* doesn't have a specific destination, but it is heading towards the Camelopardis constellation. It is estimated that *Voyager 1* will reach the constellation in the 40th millennia! (This translates as AD 40,000!)

You don't have to wait that long for the next interstellar fly-past, *Voyager 2* will fly close to the Barnard star (5.96 light years from the Sun) in AD 8,600!

Add to the diagram your own imagined space mysteries yet to be encountered by *Voyager 1* as it leaves the heliosphere ... A couple have been added for you – can you spot them?

Nearest star
Proxima Centauri
4.2 light years away

Neptune

Away from Earth

Saturn

Jupiter

Mars

Pluto

Jurassica – the
dinosaur planet

Leaving out heliosphere

Uranus

Voyager 1

Madonna – an
ageing singing star

Nearest galaxy
Canis Major
42,000 light years away

At the same time you can check out these **Things You Wish You'd Invented**:
7: Time Zones • 8: Nuclear Weapons • 10: Time Machine
13: Satellite • 31: Compass • 34: Teleporter • 72: X-ray

Microscope and Telescope

These inventions opened up whole new worlds – one tiny, the other huge. Without them, the universe wouldn't be nearly as interesting.

Teeny Weeny

The inventors of the first microscope were Dutch spectacle makers Zaccharia and Hans Janssen, around 1600. A few years later the famous inventor Galileo came up with an improved version that had a focusing device.

Anton van Leeuwenhoek (1632–1723) was the first person to devote himself to the study of really tiny things, and developed an instrument that enabled him to see bacteria and blood corpuscles. Leeuwenhoek's microscope could magnifiy objects by 270 times. Today's light microscopes allow us to see objects as small as one thousandth of a millimetre! And electron microscopes, invented in 1931 by Max Knott and Ernst Ruska, can magnify objects by several *million* times ...

Ginormous

Round about the same time as microscopes were invented, someone was busy inventing the telescope (no one's quite sure who was the first – Hans Lipperhey, James Metius or Zaccharias Janssen). Galileo (him again) got his hands on the design, improved it, and used it to discover all kinds of exciting stuff, including Jupiter's moons and the rings of Saturn.

The most powerful telescopes today are the two Keck telescopes in Hawaii. Each one is eight storeys high and weighs 300 tonnes. They don't give as clear images as the Hubble Space Telescope though, which is much smaller but orbits the Earth in space.

Microscope and Telescope **Form**

Once you have put this **Invention** to good use,
stick your Achieved Star here and fill in the form

Achieved

TEENY WEENY!

To earn your star, look at the following items under a microscope and draw a detailed
representation of what you see in the spaces provided below. If you don't have access
to a microscope, do some research on the internet or find a picture in a book.

HUMAN HAIR

AN INSECT

A DROP OF WATER

What did you discover that you couldn't see with the human eye?

GINORMOUS!

Now look at the following astronomical objects through a telescope and draw a detailed
representation of what you saw in the spaces provided below. If you don't have access
to a telescope, do some research on the internet or find a picture in a book.

THE MOON

MARS

SATURN

What did you discover that you couldn't see with the human eye?

At the same time you can check out these Things You Wish You'd Invented:
4: Cloning • 6: Photography • 13: Satellite • 40: Spectacles • 56: World Wide Web
60: Inter-Stellar Travel • 72: X-ray • 76: Intelligent Robots

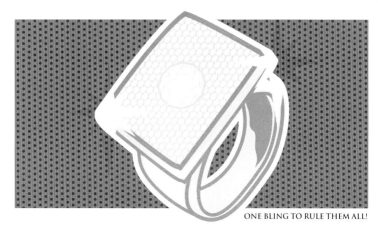

ONE BLING TO RULE THEM ALL!

Bling

If you think people wear a lot of jewellery today, you may be surprised to hear that people were even more into their bling in the past.

Good As Gold

Our ancestors were wearing necklaces and bracelets 40,000 years ago! Early jewellery was made from shells, bone, teeth and stone.

- Around 7,000 years ago, the first metal jewellery was made from copper.
- Jewellery was made in workshops in China about 5,000 years ago. The favourite ancient Chinese bling material was jade, a beautiful green stone.
- From around 5,000–4,000 years ago, rich men and women all over the Middle East loved to wear jewellery. Archaeological finds from the ancient city of Ur (in modern-day Iraq) include necklaces, bracelets and brooches made from gold, silver and semi-precious stones.
- The ancient Egyptians liked their bling too, especially made from gold. Ancient workshops made beautiful, intricate jewellery of all kinds, using gold, silver, precious stones and glass beads. Cleopatra's favourite gem-stones were supposed to have been emeralds.
- The people of the Indus Valley (the modern-day Indian subcontinent) were the first to mine diamonds around 300 BC.

We're pretty restrained in our bling compared to most ancient people. Few understood the concept of 'less is more': if you could afford it, you'd struggle along under as much precious metal, beads and stones as you could carry.

Diamonds are for ever: The first diamond miners, in the Indus Valley, prized diamonds above other jewels as we do today. But the ancient Chinese people didn't think much of them: they used them to cut jade, but not to make jewellery.

Bling **Form**

Once you have put this **Invention** to good use,
stick your Achieved Star here and fill in the form

Achieved

— RING 1 TOP VIEW — **YOU IS BLINGING!** — RING 2 TOP VIEW —

Design your own jewellery using the templates
provided here. Make it the most impressive
bling your friends have ever seen and
personalise it so it is unique to you. Once you
have finished your designs, move on to the next
stage and try to make them!

Do you have a name for your blinging collection?

Your finger
goes here

Your finger
goes here

NECKLACE

RING 1 SIDE VIEW

RING 2 SIDE VIEW

LEFT EARRING

RIGHT EARRING

BELT BUCKLE

At the same time you can check out these **Things You Wish You'd Invented:**
9: Money • 14: Playing Cards • 19: Birthdays • 37: Fashion • 40: Spectacles
45: Jeans • 51: Make-up • 75: Teenagers • 85: Mirror

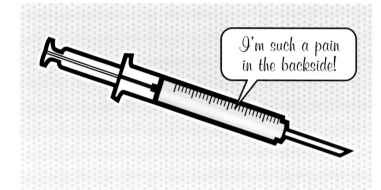

Anaesthetics

Fancy having a limb sawn off with nothing but a piece of leather to bite into to ease the pain? Probably not – but not so long ago, surgery without anaesthetic was a reality for lots of people.

It's a Knock-out

In ancient China, acupuncture was used to reduce pain and desensitise particular areas of the body. Dioscorides, a Greek doctor who lived around the first century AD, mentioned the use of drugs such as opium as anaesthetics. Alcohol was also used to deaden patients' senses. Then, in the 1800s, three different types of anaesthetic came along ...

- In 1799 Humphry Davy found that the gas nitrous oxide could make people laugh and suggested its use in surgery. He threw hilarious laughing gas parties, but the gas wasn't effective as an anaesthetic at first.
- The chemical diethyl ether was successfully used in 1846 in a tooth extraction by dentist William Morton. Morton wanted to keep it a secret but a patient forced him to reveal his methods.
- One of Queen Victoria's doctors, Sir James Young Simpson, found that a different chemical, chloroform, could be used for pain in childbirth. The queen herself used it when she gave birth in 1853, and chloroform became popular as an anaesthetic even though it's dangerous.
- Today different substances, including nitrous oxide and ether derivatives, are used in anaesthesia, which has come a long way since the 1800s.

Long before anaesthetic, as far back as the Stone Age, people all over the world practised trepanning – drilling holes in the skull. No one's sure what it was for. The earliest head-drilling operation we know about dates back 7,000 years!

Anaesthetics **Form**

Once you have put this **Invention** to good use,
stick your Achieved Star here and fill in the form

Achieved

WHERE DOES IT HURT?

On the diagrams below indicate where you've had injections before and what (if you can remember)
they were for? Using a different colour, shade the area of your body that's had to endure your most
painful experience, and when you probably really wished you could have had an anaesthetic!

MOST PAINFUL EXPERIENCE

Where was it?

How long did the pain last?

[ ] days   [ ] hours   [ ] mins

What happened?

FRONT VIEW

BACK VIEW

Injection 1

Where was it?

How painful was it? [/5]

Injection 2

Where was it?

How painful was it? [/5]

Injection 3

Where was it?

How painful was it? [/5]

Injection 4

Where was it?

How painful was it? [/5]

At the same time you can check out these **Things You Wish You'd Invented**:
48: Aspirin • 61: Microscope and Telescope • 72: X-ray • 79: Toothpaste
84: Anti-Ageing Pills • 91: Antibiotics • 95: Soap • 96: Know-It-All Hat

Umbrella

If you live in the UK you'd be very soggy a lot of the time without this simple but clever invention.

Raindrops Keep Falling on My Head

The umbrella was invented around 2000 BC in China, and not a moment too soon – it was bucketing down. Collapsible parasols, or sun shades, had been around even longer than that: the earliest evidence of a parasol is an engraving from around 2400 BC in modern-day Iraq. The Chinese seem to have been the first to have the bright idea of making them waterproof, using wax or lacquer. During the Wei Dynasty, the emperor's umbrella was red and yellow while everyone else had to have a blue one.

The Chinese invention spread to Japan, Korea, Persia and Western Europe. The first European umbrellas had ribs made from wood or whalebone and were covered with oiled canvas. In 1852 Samuel Fox, a manufacturer of women's corsets, had lots of steel corset ribs left over and came up with the idea of using them for umbrellas. It was another hundred years before the giant leap forward in umbrella design of compact collapsible umbrellas. But the basic umbrella design has stayed the same for thousands of years.

The very latest umbrellas use nanotechnology to make them bone dry after a good shake. The special umbrella fabric doesn't absorb water.

 Reigning umbrellas: The first shop to sell nothing but umbrellas was James Smith and Sons, which opened in 1830 in Foubert Street in London. It moved to New Oxford Street in 1857 and it's still there and still in business.

Umbrella **Form**

Once you have put this **Invention** to good use,
stick your Achieved Star here and fill in the form

Achieved

RAIN, RAIN, GO AWAY ...

Test your knowledge with the quiz below. Once you've completed it,
memorise the correct facts, then impress your friends to earn your star.

1. Which of the following is one of
   the wettest places on Earth?

a) Manchester, UK
b) Cherrapunjee, India
c) Emun, Burma
d) Vancouver, Canada

2. Approximately how much rainfall does
   it receive on average a year?

a) 5 m
b) 7 m
c) 9 m
d) 11 m

3. In 1952, Cilaos, on the island of
   Reunion, took the record for the
   highest rainfall ever in 24 hours.
   How much rain fell?

a) 39 cm
b) 93 cm
c) 131 cm
d) 187 cm

4. Complete the following sentence: It is
   estimated that parts of the Atacama
   desert in Chile haven't had rain for ...

a) 4 years
b) 40 years
c) 400 years
d) 4,000 years

5. On average, how many days a
   year does it rain on Mt Wai-ale-ale
   in Hawaii?

a) 275
b) 300
c) 350
d) 365 – every day of the year

6. How fast can large raindrops fall?

a) 10 mph
b) 20 mph
c) 30 mph
d) 40 mph

7. Bearing in mind how tightly
   packed the trees are in a rainforest,
   up to how long can it take for the
   rain to hit the floor?

a) About a minute
b) About 10 minutes
c) About an hour
d) Sometimes never

8. Rainforests cover ____% of the
   Earth's surface and are home to
   ____% of the Earth's plants and
   animals. Fill in the blanks with ...

a) 2% and 50%
b) 4% and 60%
c) 6% and 70%
d) 8% and 80%

9. How many African elephants,
   each weighing 5 tonnes, would
   be equivalent in weight to a
   typical cumulus cloud?

a) 1 (5 tonnes)
b) 11 (55 tonnes)
c) 110 (550 tonnes)
d) 1,110 (5,500 tonnes)

Answers at the
back of the book

At the same time you can check out these Things You Wish You'd Invented:

13: Satellite • 20: Thermometer • 23: Plastic • 69: Weather Machine • 73: Sunscreen

Gunpowder

Gunpowder is, of course, used to fire guns. But it's also used in fireworks. So it's something you might well wish you'd invented.

Whizz Bang

Gunpowder, the first manufactured explosive, is a mixture of saltpetre, sulphur and charcoal. No one knows who invented it. The earliest mention of the substance, though it's a bit vague, is in a book written by a Chinese alchemist called Wei Boyang from AD 142. Ancient Chinese alchemists are known to have conducted many experiments in the search for eternal life, and it is thought, ironically, that gunpowder may have been discovered accidentally this way.

The Chinese first used gunpowder for fireworks. But by AD 904 it was being used to make 'flying fires' in warfare. Soon they were able to produce grenades, bombs and fire missiles using gunpowder.

We don't know how gunpowder made its way from China around the world. It may have been invented independently in different places. The first mention of gunpowder in Europe was in 1216, when Roger Bacon wrote that it was possible to 'compose artificially a fire that can be launched over long distances'. By the end of the 13th century the Chinese were using gunpowder to fire their new invention, cannons. Since then gunpowder's been used in different types of guns, bombs and mortars all over the world.

The Gunpowder Plot in which Guy Fawkes and his co-conspirators planned to blow up the Houses of Parliament, may be one of the most famous uses of gunpowder. It used to be a criminal offence in England *not* to celebrate the capture of Guy Fawkes!

Gunpowder **Form**

Once you have put this **Invention** to good use,
stick your Achieved Star here and fill in the form

Achieved

GUNPOWDER PLOT

On 5 November 1605, Guy Fawkes and his accomplices attempted to blow up the Houses of Parliament while King James I and his sons were inside. The plot was uncovered and the traitors were rounded up and executed. Every 5 November since this event has been commemorated with a bonfire and the burning of an effigy of Guy Fawkes. In fact, right up until 1959, there was a law in England stating that it was illegal NOT to celebrate Guy Fawkes night. You could be arrested for not celebrating!

MAKE A GUY

WHAT YOU NEED: an old jumper, an old pair of gloves, an old pair of trousers, an old pair of socks, an old pair of tights, string, straw, newspaper, a mask

Start by taking each item of clothing and filling it up with straw and newspaper. Fill the jumper, trousers, socks and gloves until they take on the shape of parts of the body.

Now attach the items. Pull the gloves over the ends of the arms of the jumper and tie them together with string. Do the same with the socks, pulling them over the bottom of the trousers and tying them.

Then take the two halves of your guy and pull the bottom of the jumper over the top of the trousers and tie them together for extra strength.

Finally, take the tights and fill one of the legs with straw and newspaper, fashioning it into a ball shape for his head. You can either draw a face straight on to the tights or you can make a paper mask of Guy (as shown) and attach it to the head. Secure the head to the body using string.

PENNY FOR THE GUY

In the days leading up to Bonfire Night, it used to be common practice for children to cart their Guys around from house to house, asking for a penny.

It was also the custom to sing rhymes to commemorate the events of 5 November 1605. You have probably heard the rhyme below – or something like it ...

GUNPOWDER, TREASON AND PLOT

Remember, remember, the fifth
of November
Gunpowder, treason and plot.
I see no reason why gunpowder treason
Should ever be forgot.

Guy Fawkes, Guy Fawkes, 'twas his intent
To blow up the King and the parliament.
Three score barrels were laid below
To prove old England's overthrow.

By God's mercy he was catched
With a dark lantern and lighted match.
Holler boys, holler boys, let the bells ring,
Holler boys, holler boys, God save the King.

YOUR BONFIRE NIGHT

Did you make a Guy? y/n   Rate your Guy ...

What else did you get up to on Bonfire Night?

☆ Awful ☆ OK ☆ Good ☆ Great ☆ Excellent

How did you feel when you saw him burn?   Happy ☐   Sad ☐

At the same time you can check out these **Things You Wish You'd Invented:**
3: Matches • 8: Nuclear Weapons • 11: Fingerprinting • 12: Dynamite • 22: Prison

The tea leaves say:
'It's your turn to wash up!'

Tea

Did you know that people consume more tea than any other drink, apart from water? Tea might not contain much caffeine, but that hasn't stopped it from becoming highly addictive …

One Lump or Two?

We've been drinking tea in the UK for 350 years, but its history is much longer than that. According to legend, nearly 5,000 years ago a servant was boiling water for the Chinese emperor when some leaves from a nearby tea tree blew into the cup. The emperor tried the drink and invented tea. This story might seem a bit unlikely, but tea was definitely invented in China and was definitely being drunk by around 2,000 years ago (we know this because tea containers have been found from this time).

- Chinese tea-drinking became really popular from the 600s. In the 700s a whole book was written about tea, by a Chinese writer called Lu Yu.
- Tea-drinking quickly spread to Japan, but didn't arrive in Europe until about 1600, when the Dutch became the first to import tea from Java.
- By 1658 tea was being sold in Britain. It was an expensive, exotic drink in those days, and a government tax on tea kept the price high.
- In 1784 the tea tax was lowered and most people could afford a cuppa.
- A tea merchant called Thomas Sullivan invented the tea bag around 1908. First they were made from silk, later from gauze and finally from paper. Now people could make tea the lazy way.

Liber-tea! In the 1700s the British taxed tea imported to the USA. In 1773 protesting Americans raided ships and threw imported tea into the sea in what became known as the Boston Tea Party, which sparked the American Revolution.

Tea Form

Once you have put this **Invention** to good use,
stick your Achieved Star here and fill in the form

Achieved

TEA TIME

There are over 3,000 different types of tea, so rather than sticking to your usual cuppa, why not try some other varieties and see if they're better than your usual drink.

Your usual type of tea	Name of tea type 1	Name of tea type 2
A word to describe the taste	A word to describe the taste	A word to describe the taste
Overall rating	Overall rating	Overall rating
1 2 3 4 5	1 2 3 4 5	1 2 3 4 5

Name of tea type 3	Name of tea type 4	Name of tea type 5
A word to describe the taste	A word to describe the taste	A word to describe the taste
Overall rating	Overall rating	Overall rating
1 2 3 4 5	1 2 3 4 5	1 2 3 4 5

Name of tea type 6	Name of tea type 7	Name of tea type 8
A word to describe the taste	A word to describe the taste	A word to describe the taste
Overall rating	Overall rating	Overall rating
1 2 3 4 5	1 2 3 4 5	1 2 3 4 5

VERDICT

Did you prefer any of the other teas to your usual? y/n

Did you add sugar to improve the taste? y/n

Which was your least favourite?

If yes, which one?

Will you be drinking this one from now on? y/n

Did you finish the cup? y/n

At the same time you can check out these **Things You Wish You'd Invented**:
5: Fast Food • 18: Fizzy Drinks • 27: Pizza • 32: Cutlery
43: Sliced Bread • 68: Refrigerator • 97: Alcoholic Drinks

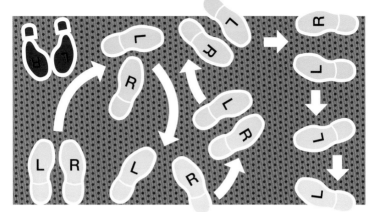

The Dad Dance

Dancing

How glad you are about the invention of dancing will depend largely on whether or not you're any good at it.

Dancing Queen

Of course, no one knows who was the first person to start tapping their feet in time to some music or the site of the world's first dance floor. But we can safely say that dancing has been around for a very, very long time.

- At Bhimbekta in India, Stone Age rock paintings more than 9,000 years old show scenes of people dancing.
- Rock carvings at Alta in Norway more than 6,000 years old also show dancing scenes, and so do Egyptian tomb paintings more than 5,000 years old.
- The Minoans of ancient Crete (around 5,000 to 3,400 years ago) were keen on dancing and have left sculptures of dancing figures, as well as paintings of dancers, to prove it. According to Minoan mythology, the goddess Rea taught humans to dance.
- The ancient Greeks took dancing very seriously and made it a basic part of their education system.
- The very first dances might have been used as part of religious rituals, or to tell stories, or a combination of both. But you only have to look at a baby's response to music to realise that dancing comes naturally – though some people lose their sense of rhythm once they grow up.

Morris dancing is a type of English folk dancing that's been around since the Middle Ages. Traditionally, it's danced by men wearing white costumes with bells on their legs. They might wave hankies, tobacco pipes, sticks or even blown-up pigs' bladders.

Dancing **Form**

Once you have put this **Invention** to good use,
stick your Achieved Star here and fill in the form

Achieved

———————————— LET'S DANCE ————————————

Invent a brand-new dance! Think up nine moves and choose the best song to perform it to.
Draw or describe your nine moves in the spaces provided below. When you're happy with
your routine, give it a name, then show it to the rest of the family or your friends to earn
your star. Give yourself an extra star if you can get them to join in!

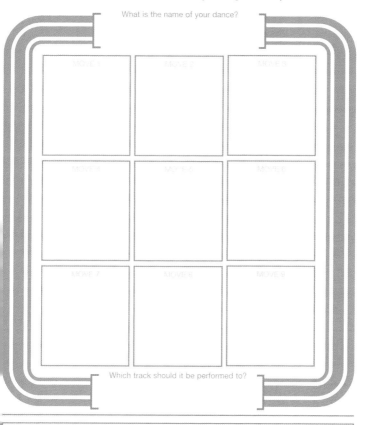

What is the name of your dance?

MOVE 1	MOVE 2	MOVE 3
MOVE 4	MOVE 5	MOVE 6
MOVE 7	MOVE 8	MOVE 9

Which track should it be performed to?

At the same time you can check out these **Things You Wish You'd Invented:**
19: Birthdays • 21: Guitar • 25: Poetry • 35: CDs and DVDs • 46: Music
56: World Wide Web • 75: Teenagers • 85: Mirror

Refrigerator

Next time you reach for a cold can of Coke, spare a thought for the millions of people who lived before fridges were invented.

Keeping Cool

Keeping food cool keeps it fresher for longer. Since food that isn't fresh can kill you, this is very important. Before fridges, people put food in cold, dark, damp places, or in a hole packed with ice or snow. Artificial cooling started more than 250 years ago ...

- In 1748 William Cullen demonstrated how freezing temperatures could be obtained by evaporating ether. But he didn't use it to build a fridge.
- Oliver Evans, an American inventor, proposed a refrigeration machine in 1805 that used compressed ether, but he never developed the idea.
- Jacob Perkins was the first person to actually build a machine that cooled things down. He patented his invention in 1834.
- The first commercial refrigerators were used in the brewing and meat-packing industries in Australia and the USA in the 1850s. Improvements in the design led to the first domestic fridges going on sale in 1913.

Until 1929 fridges used poisonous gases ammonia, methyl chloride and sulphur dioxide, which caused several deaths. After that Freon was used – a compound invented by two scientists called Charles Franklin and Thomas Medgeley, Jr, and manufactured by Du Pont. It was much safer, but years late people realised that the chlorofluorocarbons in Freon were destroying the Earth's ozone layer!

Relatively cold: Albert Einstein came up with all sorts of clever things. Not many people know that one of them was a fridge, which he invented in partnership with a former student, Leo Szilard. They took out a patent in 1930.

Refrigerator **Form**

Once you have put this **Invention** to good use, stick your Achieved Star here and fill in the form

Achieved

MAKE ICE CREAM

The ice-cream-making process takes a lot of time, but the results are well worth it. Ask an adult to be your assistant.

WHAT YOU NEED

a big bowl, a saucepan, wooden spoons, a fridge, a freezer

INGREDIENTS: 4 egg yolks, 1/2 pint (250 ml) milk, 1/2 pint (250 ml) double cream, 4 oz (100 g) sugar or caster sugar, 2 teaspoons of vanilla extract (or more according to taste)

STEP A

Put the egg yolks and the sugar into a big bowl and stir until the mixture gets thicker.

Pour the milk into a saucepan and bring it to the boil. Then add the the milk to your sugar and egg mixture, but keep stirring at all times.

When thoroughly mixed, pour the liquid back into the saucepan and heat gently, stirring all the time until the mixture thickens. IMPORTANT – DO NOT BOIL. Once thickened, remove the saucepan from the heat and leave to cool.

STEP B

The mixture you have made is the basis for all ice-cream flavours. Add the vanilla essence now if you want vanilla ice cream, but at this point you can create any flavour you like – so experiment (check out www.ice-cream-recipes.com)

When your mixture is cool, you could put it into an ice-cream maker for an easy life, but if you haven't got one, pour the mixture into a plastic food container and chill it for a few hours in the fridge. Then stir in the double cream and transfer the mixture to the freezer for half an hour. The ice cream should have started to freeze – but you don't want it to be fully frozen as you have to beat it.

Beat the mixture until there are no lumps and it becomes liquid again, then return it to the freezer, beating it again half an hour later. Repeat this process three times and your ice cream should be ready to eat.

FLAVOUR OF THE MONTH

Which flavours have you made?

☐ Vanilla	☐ Strawberry	☐ Chocolate
☐ Honey	☐ Mint Choc	☐ Blueberry
☐ Choc Chip	☐ Stem Ginger	☐ Pistachio
☐ Toffee	☐ Lemon	☐ Banana
☐ Peanut Butter	☐ Chilli	☐ Your flavour

TASTE TEST

How good is your ice cream?

☆ ☆ ☆ ☆ ☆

UUurrrgh!!   Hmmm?   Ah!!!!   Mmmm!!!   Yummy!!!!

ICE-CREAM ROULETTE

Here is a way to make mischief. Why not make six different ice-cream dishes and make one of them a nasty flavour? For instance, you could have five great flavours such as: chocolate, vanilla, strawberry, banana and mint choc chip, and then one really nasty flavour – like tomato ketchup or mustard flavour.

Bring your ice creams to the table when they're ready. Serve them into identical dishes and place them on a tray. Now invite your guests in.

It's time to spin the tray. When it stops spinning each person must take the flavour that ends up in front of them, but try to make sure you don't get the tomato ketchup flavour! Leave that one for Dad!

At the same time you can check out these **Things You Wish You'd Invented**:
5: Fast Food • 18: Fizzy Drinks • 20: Thermometer
27: Pizza • 43: Sliced Bread • 79: Toothpaste

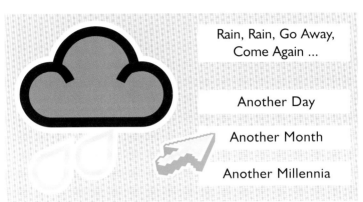

Rain, Rain, Go Away,
Come Again ...

Another Day

Another Month

Another Millennia

Weather Machine

The weather has always been difficult to predict, and scientists say we can expect more freak weather conditions as global warming takes its toll. At the moment, we're lucky just to have an accurate prediction for a few days in advance. We could really do with a device to tell the weather what to do!

Under the Weather

If a machine to organise the weather did exist then summers could be full of glorious sunshine, and winters could guarantee snow – it'd be wonderful! But you couldn't just forget about the rest of the weather. Without rain, plants won't grow and our water reserves would soon be stretched. Here are some ideas as to how to use your machine:

- The way to get around the lack of rain would be to arrange for it to rain regularly at night, when most people are asleep in bed.
- If you wanted to get out of your sports day, you could program the machine to rain all day! Or if you needed a few more days to revise for your end-of-year exams, you could make it snow heavily in June. No one would suspect you – they'd blame the freak weather on climate change.
- Put an end to Christmas Days without snow and rainy bank holidays!
- If you'd always wanted to see a tornado, you could just summon one up – although you'd have to do it somewhere safe, away from populated areas.
- You could even help prevent some of the worst effects of global warming by keeping the weather really cold around the ice caps, and making it rain in areas of the world severely affected by drought.

To really command the weather, you'd need to be able to control the Earth's tilt on its axis and its orbit around the Sun. These factors lie behind seasonal changes, and explain why it's winter in the northern hemisphere when it's summer in the southern hemisphere, and vice versa.

Weather Machine **Form**

Once you have put this **Invention** to good use,
stick your Achieved Star here and fill in the form

Achieved

--------------------- **WHATEVER THE WEATHER** ---------------------

What would be your perfect day weather-wise? Take a look at the chart below and construct
the ideal weather conditions.

Which is your favourite season?

Spring ☐   Summer ☐   Autumn ☐   Winter ☐

How do you like your sun?

☐ Full blast, cloudless

☐ Mainly sunny with a little cloud

☐ Half sunny, half cloudy

☐ Hidden behind clouds

How do you like your rain?

☐ No rain at all

☐ A little shower here and there

☐ Heavy downpours

☐ Constant, driving rain

How do you like your wind?

0 ☐ No wind at all

5 ☐ A little whisper now and then

10 ☐ A brisk breeze

25 ☐ Strong and gusty!

How do you like your snow?

☐ No snow at all

☐ A little snow here and there

☐ Mixed with rain to make sleet

☐ Heavy snow

Other conditions

☐ °C I like it cold!

☐ °C I like it hot

☐ I like thunder and lightning

☐ I like extreme weather

At the same time you can check out these **Things You Wish You'd Invented:**
20: Thermometer • 24: Hot-Air Balloon • 41: Football
64: Umbrella • 73: Sunscreen • 90: Maps • 100: Chindogu • 101: Room 101

Fireworks

New Year's Eve and Bonfire Night would be so much less exciting, colourful and noisy without the invention of fireworks.

Gone in a Flash

The earliest type of firework was invented about 2,000 years ago in China, when it was discovered that freshly cut bamboo thrown on to a fire causes a rather loud explosion. People were soon throwing bamboo on fires to ward off evil spirits. Then the Chinese invented gunpowder (see **Invention** No. 65) and some bright spark had the idea to press this explosive mixture into the bamboo tubes. The invention of the firecracker, around 1,000 years ago, has been credited to a monk called Li Tian, who packed the gunpowder mixture into paper tubes. The Chinese continued to develop fireworks as they became a popular form of entertainment, and by the 13th century Europe had got in on the act. Queen Elizabeth I liked them so much that she created the position of 'Fire Master of England'. James II knighted his Fire Master.

Ancient Chinese fireworks weren't multi-coloured: they were all yellow. They had to rely on amazing shapes and loud bangs to make them spectacular and exciting. It wasn't until 1800 that a French chemist called Claude Berthollet discovered potassium chlorate, which made different coloured fireworks possible. Today fireworks continue to be enjoyed all over the world, and China is still the biggest manufacturer and exporter of them.

Firework face-off: If you want to see a really amazing firework display, go to the next World Pyro Olympics, where firework companies from all over the world compete against one another in a five-day competition.

Fireworks **Form**

Once you have put this **Invention** to good use,
stick your Achieved Star here and fill in the form

Achieved

── LET'S CELEBRATE! ──

Fireworks are used in celebrations all over the world. Here is a list of some of the biggest ones.
Tick the boxes and earn your star if you've taken part in an event to celebrate the following dates.

UNITED KINGDOM, BONFIRE NIGHT

On 5 November 1605, Guy Fawkes, together with the other conspirators in the
'Gunpowder Plot', attempted to blow up James I and the Houses of Parliament.
The plot was uncovered and the perpertrators were executed. So Bonfire Night
is actually a celebration of something that never actually happened!

Have you ever been to a
celebration of this event?   Were there fireworks?

UNITED STATES, INDEPENDENCE DAY

On 4 July 1776, the Declaration of Independence was signed, marking the
beginning of self-government in the USA, and independence from Great Britain.
It has been celebrated every year since with a national holiday and patriotic
displays.

Have you ever been to a
celebration of this event?   Were there fireworks?

CHINA, CHINESE NEW YEAR

Chinese New Year is the most important celebration in the Chinese calendar and
the party goes on for 15 days! The date is based on the first day of the new year
containing a new moon, and so it changes every year due to the phases of the
Moon. It usually falls either at the end of January or the beginning of February.

Have you ever been to a
celebration of this event?   Were there fireworks?

INDIA, DIWALI

Diwali is a five-day Hindu festival that celebrates the triumph of good over evil.
It occurs on the 15th day of the Hindu calendar month of Kartika, which falls
between mid-October and mid-November. It is also known as the 'Festival of
Lights' because of the use of small oil lamps to decorate buildings.

Have you ever been to a
celebration of this event?   Were there fireworks?

ALL OVER THE WORLD, NEW YEAR'S EVE

New Year's Eve is celebrated on 31 December by the countries that use the
Gregorian calendar of 365/366 days. It is the largest party in the world, and
although other countries observe their own traditions, fireworks at midnight
is a custom adopted by almost all of them.

Have you ever been to a
celebration of this event?   Were there fireworks?

At the same time you can check out these **Things You Wish You'd Invented**:
3: Matches • 12: Dynamite • 19: Birthdays • 30: Magic
41: Football • 64 Umbrella • 69. Weather Machine • 81: Laser

Numbers

Imagine a world without numbers: you wouldn't know how much money you had and when you spent it you'd have no idea how much anything cost. On the other hand, you wouldn't have to do quadratic equations.

Think of a Number ...

The earliest evidence of numbers ever found – tally marks scored into stone – dates from more than 30,000 years ago. Making marks on stone or wood is all very well if you just want to keep a note of small numbers, but if you want to use bigger numbers, you need a system. For example, without a system the number 23 would look something like this: ///////////////////// (i.e. not very useful). But because we're working on the decimal system, we put a 2 in the left-hand column to signify two lots of ten, and a 3 in the right-hand column to signify three lots of one.

The first people to use a number system were the ancient Mesopotamians, around 3400 BC. Unlike our decimal system (base ten), the Mesopotamians had a sexagesimal system (base 60). They probably liked the number 60 because so many other numbers divide evenly into it. The number 23 in the decimal system means two lots of ten and three lots of one, but for an ancient Mesopotamian the number would mean two lots of sixty and three lots of one – 123 in the decimal system. We have the ancient Egyptians to thank for the earliest example of the decimal system, which dates to about 3100 BC and which means we don't have to multiply by 60 all the time.

Zero tolerance: The 1 to 9 digits we use today were developed in India by Aryabhata I about AD 500. In the 800s Persian mathematician Muhammad ibn Musa al-Khwarizmi was among the first to establish the idea of using a 0 to show powers of ten (10, 100, 1,000 etc.)

Numbers **Form**

Once you have put this **Invention** to good use,
stick your Achieved Star here and fill in the form

Achieved

--- **SUDOKU** ---

It's everyone's favourite numbers game! Try your hand at the sudoku puzzles below. There is an easy, medium and hard puzzle to solve and once you've completed them try to create your own sudoku puzzle. HOW TO PLAY: Complete the grid so that each column, row and 3x3 grid contain the numbers 1 to 9, without repeating any of those numbers. In case you've never played it before, it's a game of logic and you'll be pleased to hear no maths is involved! YOUR PUZZLE: Filling in the grid with the numbers is the easiest bit. Trying to figure out which numbers to leave out to make it into a puzzle is the hard part.

PUZZLE 1

	7	5		9	8	4	2	
	2					9		
	8		2					5
7		3	6		2			
	1	9			7			
2	5	6	4		1	9	8	
3			8	5		6	1	
		4						8
				6	5	7	4	

PUZZLE 2

5		3	8				4	6
				3				1
8	4	1				9	7	
1	7	6	5				2	4
3	8			2				7
			1			3		
			6		4			
	7					4	1	
			7		5			9

PUZZLE 3

6				2			7	
	9		7					
3		1	9	8	6	4	2	
			8			9		7
			2	3	9	1		
8			5	1	7			
5		8				6		
9	4		6	5			3	8
	3							

YOUR PUZZLE

(blank grid)

At the same time you can check out these **Things You Wish You'd Invented:**
2: Mobile Phones • 9: Money • 14: Playing Cards • 19: Birthdays
29: Post-It Notes • 30: Magic • 42: School • 49: Homework Machine • 88: Computer

X-ray

Since X-ray machines were invented, doctors have been able to see exactly which bone is broken or fractured and where. Before that, the only way to see inside the body was to cut it open – which is quite a lot more painful than taking an X-ray.

X-ray Specs

X-rays are part of the electromagnetic spectrum – like radio waves, or light. They were discovered in 1895. German scientist Wilhelm Rontgen was experimenting with electron beams and noticed that they could pass through cardboard and other materials on to a screen. When he put his hand in front of the generator, an image of the bones inside his hand appeared on the screen. By chance, he'd discovered a new kind of radiation, which he referred to as 'X'. The first X-ray image ever taken was of Rontgen's wife's hand.

X-rays allow us to see through skin and the squishy bits inside our bodies to the bones because the skin and squishy bits are made up of smaller atoms, which don't absorb X-ray photons very well. The calcium atoms bones are made of are bigger, so they do absorb the photons and show up on X-rays.

Today, a combination of X-rays, ultrasound and magnetic resonance (using radio waves) provides amazing 3-D images of our insides – the bones and the squishy bits too.

 Danger-rays: X-rays are a lot less dangerous and less messy than cutting open the body, but it wasn't realised that X-rays are dangerous in a different way until years after they were discovered. Too much exposure to them can cause cancer.

X-ray Form

Once you have put this **Invention** to good use,
stick your Achieved Star here and fill in the form

Achieved

X-RAY VISION

Have you ever had an X-ray? On the diagram below, colour in the areas you've had
X-rayed and fill in the form with more information about your experiences with X-ray.

X-ray area 1

Why did you have this X-ray?

What happened next?

X-ray area 2

Why did you have this X-ray?

What happened next?

X-ray area 3

Why did you have this X-ray?

What happened next?

At the same time you can check out these Things You Wish You'd Invented:
4: Cloning • 6: Photography • 8: Nuclear Weapons • 30: Magic • 48: Aspirin
60: Inter-Stellar Travel • 63: Anaesthetics • 81: Laser • 91: Antibiotics

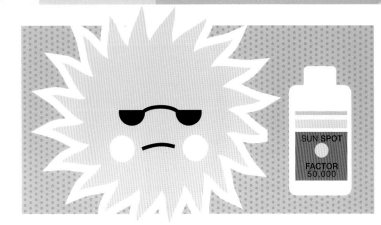

Sunscreen

Today, most people with white skin use sunscreens – at least, they should. These block sunburn-causing UVB rays and the best ones also protect against UVA rays, which can cause long-term sun damage.

Here Comes the Sun

Effective sunscreens were only invented in the 20th century. That's probably because people didn't sunbathe until the 1920s – before that, the fashion for pale skin meant that people kept out of the sun, unless they worked outside, in which case they had to resign themselves to being deeply unfashionable.

In the 1920s French fashion designer Coco Chanel came back from holiday with a suntan and started a fashion for foreign holidays and tanned skin, which became a symbol of wealth, just as pale skin had been in the past. The sun-bathers of the 1920s weren't aware of the dangers and, if they applied anything to their skin, it was to help get a suntan and not to protect themselves.

In 1938 an Austrian chemistry student called by Franz Greiter, who had suffered bad sunburn climbing Piz Buin, developed a sunscreen with an SPF of 2. Eugene Schneller, founder of L'Oreal, was also inventing sun creams in the 1930s. In 1944 Benjamin Greene invented a sticky red goo to protect Second World War soldiers from sunburn that he tested on his own bald head – it worked, but it wasn't popular with sunbathers for obvious reasons. Now, very effective sunscreens are available that aren't red and sticky.

 Sun Protection Factor: Bottles of sunscreen all show an SPF number, which indicates the length of time you can stay in the sun without burning: if your skin burns after 10 minutes, using an SPF of 10 you can stay in the sun for 100 minutes.

Sunscreen **Form**

Once you have put this **Invention** to good use,
stick your Achieved Star here and fill in the form

Achieved

HERE COMES THE SUN

Everyone should be well aware by now of the dangers of unprotected exposure to the Sun's UV rays, but how much do we really know about that great burning ball in the sky? Test your knowledge with the quiz below. Once you've completed it, memorise the correct facts, then impress your friends to earn your star. Answers at the back of the book.

1. In astronomical terms, how big is the Sun compared to other stars?

a) Small
b) Medium
c) Large
d) Extra large

2. How much of our solar system's mass is made up by the Sun?

a) 65%
b) 76%
c) 87%
d) 98%

3. What is the temperature at the Sun's core?

a) 1,500 °C
b) 1.5 million °C
c) 15 million °C
d) 150 million °C

4. Which of the following substances is not found in the Sun?

a) Iron
b) Gold
c) Carbon
d) Helium

5. How many Earths could fit into the Sun?

a) One hundred
b) One thousand
c) One hundred thousand
d) One million

6. Finish the sentence: The Sun has enough hydrogen fuel left to burn for approximately another ...

a) 1 billion years
b) 5 billion years
c) 10 billion years
d) 15 billion years

7. Approximately how old is the Sun?

a) 1 billion years old
b) 1.5 billion years old
c) 4 billion years old
d) 4.5 billion years old

8. How long does it take the Sun to rotate?

a) Approximately 9 days
b) Approximately 18 days
c) Approximately 27 days
d) Approximately 36 days

9. Which of the following statements is true?

a) Every eleven years the Sun's North and South magnetic poles swap places
b) Sunspots are areas on the Sun's surface that are lower in temperature
c) The Sun is a nuclear reactor
d) All of the above

10. Roughly how long does it take light from the Sun to reach the Earth?

a) 1 hour 4 minutes
b) 32 minutes
c) 16 minutes
d) 8 minutes

At the same time you can check out these **Things You Wish You'd Invented**:
20: Thermometer • 64: Umbrella • 69: Weather Machine
84: Anti-Ageing Pills • 87: Passport • 94: Flip Flops

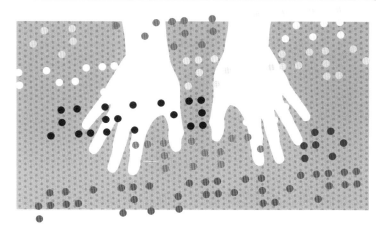

Braille

Louis Braille is a hero to millions of blind people all over the world, but not many people know that we also have Napoleon Bonaparte to thank for the invention of Braille.

Seeing Spots

Braille is a system of raised dots that can be read using touch alone. Before it was invented, there were a few books produced to teach blind people to read using embossed letters, but they were difficult and expensive to produce.

Louis Braille, who'd been blind since he was three, read some of these books when he was sent to the Royal Institute for Blind Youth in Paris. While he was there an army officer, Charles Barbier, visited the Institute and demonstrated an invention that he called 'night writing'. French general Napoleon Bonaparte had had the idea of a code that could be read at night and challenged his army to invent one. So Barbier had come up with a system that allowed soldiers to communicate silently and in total darkness using a system of raised dots to represent the alphabet. Unfortunately, Barbier's night writing was so complicated that none of the soldiers had been able to learn it.

Although Louis Braille was just 11 years old at the time, he saw the potential of Barbier's dot system straight away. He spent the next six years simplifying it and in 1821 came up with an alphabet of raised dots arranged in rectangles that could be read quickly and easily.

Visually-impaired geniuses: These include Horatio Nelson (British admiral), David Blunkett (UK politician), Eduard Degas and Claude Monet (French painters), Stevie Wonder and Ray Charles (US singer/songwriters), and Cupid/Eros (Roman/Greek god of love).

Braille **Form**

Once you have put this **Invention** to good use,
stick your Achieved Star here and fill in the form

Achieved

THE BRAILLE ALPHABET

Braille is a series of raised dots representing the letters of the alphabet that a blind or partially sighted person can read by moving their finger from left to right over the dots. Each letter is made up of up to six dots, comprised of two columns of three. To earn your star, teach yourself to read the Braille alphabet by sight, and then transfer your new skill to the power of touch by going out and finding real Braille to read with your fingertips!

TOP TIP: To help you learn Braille more quickly, it's useful to know that the letters A to J only use the top four dots, K to T all use the bottom left dot and U to Z (with the exception of W) all use the bottom two dots.

A/1   B/2   C/3   D/4   E/5   F/6   G/7   H/8   I/9   J/0   K

L   M   N   O   P   Q   R   S   T   U   V

W   X   Y   Z

As you can see, the numbers 1 to 9 and 0 are the same as A to J. So how do you know if you should be reading letters or numbers? Well, we use another symbol (see right). This symbol precedes any number.

There are many other symbols in Braille, including full stops and question marks, but try to master these basic ones first before you take on any more.

Using the alphabet above, try to read Braille by sight. What does this sentence say?

Now go and find some signs in Braille and attempt to read them! Make sure you take this book along with you so you can look up the letters!

Where did you find words in Braille?

In a museum	In a library	On food / pill packaging	On paper currency	Other

If other, where did you find Braille?

After you've read Braille with your eyes, try to read it with your finger. Familiarise yourself with the feeling of Braille and take it slowly, because if you miss one bump then a word could take on a whole new meaning or make no sense at all!

How did you get on with reading raised Braille?

I understood all of it!		I understood a few words	
It felt like random bumps		I cheated and read it in English	

Did you find learning to read
Braille difficult?   y/n

Have you got the hang of it
without the use of your sight?   y/n

What was the first sentence you read in Braille?

At the same time you can check out these **Things You Wish You'd Invented**:

17: Morse Code • 38: Sign Language • 52: Language • 78: Language Decoder

Teenagers

How could teenagers have been invented? And, no doubt, some uncharitable people might even ask 'why' ...

Uncouth Youth

Obviously, no one used to miss out the years between 13 and 19. However, until the 1950s the term 'teenagers' had never been used – musician Bill Haley is supposed to have been the first person to use the word in 1952. Before that they were 'young adults' or 'youths' and were expected to behave pretty much as adults did.

The Second World War had been rather miserable, for obvious reasons, but during the 1950s rationing ended and everyone had a bit more spare cash. New films, TV shows and especially music appealed to the young, who began to create their own style, quite different from grown-ups'.

For the first time, young people had money to spend on luxuries, and they used it to make themselves as different as possible from their parents. They listened to the new 'rock and roll' music – absolutely shocking, as you'll probably agree – and they dressed in clothes that their mums and dads definitely wouldn't be wearing. One popular teenage fashion, the 'Teds' look, made teenagers stand out rather: boys wore drainpipe trousers, long brightly coloured jackets, greasy hair with a huge quiff at the front and chunky sideburns. Teenage fashions have changed a bit since then.

 Teddy boys: The 1950s' Teds surprisingly took their inspiration from upper-class men of 50 years before, the Edwardians. Hence the name (Ted is short for Edward). By the 1960s, many Teds, especially those with motorbikes, became Rockers.

Teenagers **Form**

Once you have put this **Invention** to good use,
stick your Achieved Star here and fill in the form

Achieved

──────────── **SWEET TEEN** ────────────

When people grow up they often forget what it's like to be a teenager, even when they have
children of their own. Don't make the same mistake! Use the space below to list the important
things that should never be forgotten. Keep a record for yourself to look back on later in life.
Be honest in your answers.

Today's date

| d | d | m | m | y | y | y | y |

Your age | 0 | 0 |

Five things you love

1.

2.

3.

4.

5.

Five things you hate

1.

2.

3.

4.

5.

How do you feel about your appearance?

How do you feel about your school?

How do you feel about your friends?

How do you feel about your parents?

How do you feel about the state of the country?

How do you feel about the state of the world?

How do you feel about your future?

What makes you angry?

What makes you happy?

Describe your general sense of well being

What advice have you got for your future self?

At the same time you can check out these **Things You Wish You'd Invented:**
2: Mobile Phone • 19: Birthdays • 21: Guitar • 37: Fashion • 42: School • 45: Jeans
46: Music • 51: Make-up • 56: World Wide Web • 62: Bling • 88: Computer

Intelligent Robots

Wouldn't it be great to have your very own robot to do all the tasks you hate without complaining? Say goodbye to homework and washing-up!

Inventing a Brain

Intelligent robots don't yet exist, but today's robots can do all sorts of things: they work on assembly lines in factories, defuse bombs, vacuum the carpet, mow the lawn, and sample and analyse the surface of other planets. Different types of robot look and behave very differently from one another, so it's difficult to define what a robot is. Broadly, you could say that all robots have a computer (a brain) that controls a physical structure (a body).

But could a man-made machine ever be intelligent in the way that you are – capable of thought processes that enable it to learn, plan, have ideas and preferences? Artificially intelligent machines do already exist: computers can solve problems, as long as they're programmed to do so, and some modern robots can learn, in a limited way. But they're not likely to help with an essay on the Napoleonic Wars.

Some scientists don't believe that a truly intelligent robot will ever exist because we'll never understand how our brains work well enough to create intelligence artificially. Others believe that research into artificial intelligence will lead to machines that can think for themselves ... and eventually turn us all into human/machine hybrids.

The Honda Motor Company's ASIMO robot, which looks a bit like a small person in a spacesuit, is the most advanced humanoid robot in the world. It can walk, climb stairs, understand spoken commands, recognise faces and perform a variety of simple tasks.

Intelligent Robots **Form**

Once you have put this **Invention** to good use,
stick your Achieved Star here and fill in the form

Achieved

SLAVE TO LOVE

Robots are currently being developed across the world for domestic use, but it is going to be a long time before there will be one in every home. What kind of robot would you build?

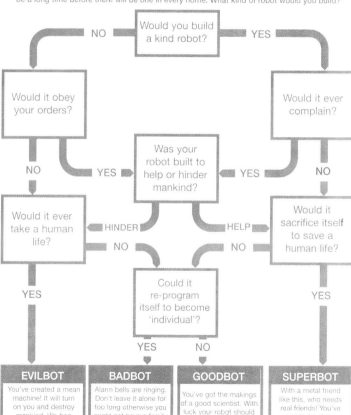

NO — Would you build a kind robot? — YES

Would it obey your orders?

Would it ever complain?

Was your robot built to help or hinder mankind?

NO — YES — help or hinder — YES — NO

Would it ever take a human life?

HINDER

HELP

Would it sacrifice itself to save a human life?

NO — NO

YES

Could it re-program itself to become 'individual'?

YES

YES — NO

EVILBOT
You've created a mean machine! It will turn on you and destroy mankind. We beg you to reconsider!

BADBOT
Alarm bells are ringing. Don't leave it alone for too long otherwise you might not have a family to go back to.

GOODBOT
You've got the makings of a good scientist. With luck your robot should behave itself ...

SUPERBOT
With a metal friend like this, who needs real friends! You've created a shiny superbeing!

At the same time you can check out these **Things You Wish You'd Invented**
8: Nuclear Weapons • 10: Time Machine • 13: Satellite • 49: Homework Machine
69: Weather Machine • 81: Laser • 98: Terraforming • 100: Chindogu

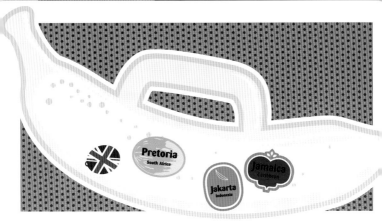

Banana Suitcase

How many times have you wished you had a specially designed holder to transport your bananas?

'Ave a Banana!

Bananas are wonderful fruit in many ways: they're delicious, low in calories, high in potassium, vitamin B6 and magnesium, and can help lower cholesterol. They come in convenient bunches, and, perhaps most obvious, each banana has its own protective thick skin.

However, someone has decided that the world is crying out for more effective banana protection. Apparently, banana skins aren't enough on their own and an extra layer of protection is needed to avoid bruising. A patent was granted for the 'Banana Protective Device' in 2003. It's a hinged, lockable case, shaped (as you'd expect) like a banana, and comes complete with interior cushioning. The inventor's instructions carefully explain how to use it: 'In use, the user opens the container and places a banana inside thereof and closes the container to allow the user to carry the banana in a safe manner.'

The next time you're transporting a banana, you might want to consider spending around £5 on a banana suitcase, which are available to buy in five different colours. There will, of course, be rogue bananas that don't fit inside the suitcase, so you'd better make sure that yours is a conventionally shaped banana before you buy. On the other hand, you might not want to bother.

The next time you reach for a bunch of bananas, watch out for spiders. The Brazilian wandering spider, or banana spider, is one of the most deadly spiders in the world. It's been known to lurk in bunches of bananas and bite unsuspecting harvesters.

Banana Suitcase **Form**

Once you have put this **Invention** to good use,
stick your Achieved Star here and fill in the form

Achieved

READY-SLICED BANANAS

Fool your school friends with a ready-sliced banana! When you take your banana out of your bag at lunchtime, before you open it, tell your friends that your parents have bought a bunch of the best bananas around. Tell them the bananas were very expensive because they are the first in a new variety of ready-sliced bananas (they won't believe you). When they challenge you to show them, peel the banana to reveal your revolution in fruit science!

WHAT TO DO

All you need for this trick is a banana and a pin.

1. Holding the banana at one end, stick the pin in the 'seam' of the banana.

2. Once the pin is almost all the way in (don't push it all the way through, and keep your fingers well out of the way just in case), wiggle it left and right. This will slice through the banana.

3. Repeat this at several points along the 'seam' of the banana. Now the banana will be in slices when you open it!

WARNING:

You should prepare your banana only a short time before performing this trick, otherwise the banana will start to go brown.

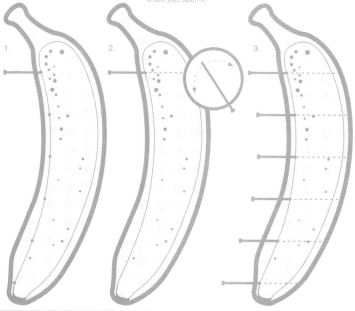

At the same time you can check out these **Things You Wish You'd Invented:**
5: Fast Food • 18: Fizzy Drinks • 23: Plastic • 27: Pizza • 32: Cutlery
43: Sliced Bread • 66: Tea • 68: Refrigerator • 100: Chindogu

LANGUAGE DECODER

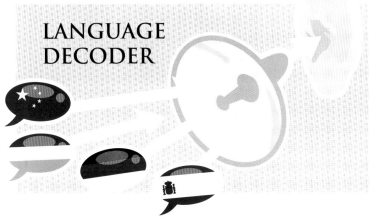

Language Decoder

A language decoder would be an incredible tool to have at your disposal – you'd be able to converse with everyone, no matter where they came from and what language they spoke! It may sound like science fiction, but the US Defence Advanced Research Projects Agency (DARPA) is working on a version of this very invention, for use by soldiers.

Found in Translation

There are over 6,000 languages spoken in the world and a good language decoder would be able to identify all of them (or at least the top 300!). The computer would probably be in headset form, so that it could work in two ways: translating what you hear *and* what you say. Think of the advantages ...

- There would be no more need for frantic pointing or repeating yourself loudly in your attempt to be understood when you're on holiday in foreign climes. Asking for directions would be a doddle – you could even have deep conversations with the locals about culture and politics!
- There would be no need for film or TV subtitles any more.
- The world would be a more peaceful place, with fewer cultural misunderstandings and breakdowns in communication.

On the downside, the more popular the device became, the more translators that would be put out of work! However, for the moment, their jobs are safe, as it looks like language decoders are still a fair way off.

Babel Fish are language decoders in Douglas Adam's *Hitchhiker's Guide to the Galaxy* books. They sit in the ear and feed off the brainwaves of other people, excreting those frequencies into your ear so that you can understand what they're saying, whatever the language.

Language Decoder **Form**

Once you have put this **Invention** to good use,
stick your Achieved Star here and fill in the form

Achieved

¿USTED ENTIENDE?

How good is your knowledge of foreign languages? Figure out what language each of the phrases
below is in, draw the flag of that nation, and then find out what the phrases means to earn your star.

LANGUAGE	NATIONAL FLAG	TRANSLATION
What language is this?	Draw the correct flag below	What did the message say?

Amo a mi madre
_____

What language is this?   Draw the correct flag below   What did the message say?

昨 天 我 的
宠 物 猫 丢 了
_____

What language is this?   Draw the correct flag below   What did the message say?

Mein Lehrer ist
ein Außerirdische
_____

What language is this?   Draw the correct flag below   What did the message say?

Nem beszélek
magyarul
_____

At the same time you can check out these **Things You Wish You'd Invented:**
13: Satellite • 17: Morse Code • 35: CDs and DVDs • 38: Sign Language
42: School • 52: Language • 74: Braille • 96: Know-It-All Hat

Toothpaste

In the past, people's mouths could be rather unpleasant places – not least because of what they put in them to try to keep them clean!

Open Wide

The ancient Egyptians used a tooth powder containing ash, egg shells and pumice stone. Worse still, ancient Roman toothpaste and mouthwash contained Portuguese urine, which they believed was the strongest kind. We still use ammonia (the whitening agent in pee) in toothpaste, but you'll be glad to hear that it's made in a laboratory.

Since then all kinds of ingredients have been used. One recipe from the 1800s contained burnt bread, and it was common for brick or china dust to be found in toothpaste in those days too. A dentist called Peabody was probably the first to add soap to toothpowder in 1824, and Glycerine was also added around this time to turn the powders into paste.

Toothpaste was sold in jars until 1892 when Dr Sheffield's Creme Dentrice became available in a tube. Dr Sheffield went on to set up Colgate.

Toothbrush

The earliest toothbrushes were sticks chewed at one end – some have been found in China from 5,000 years ago.

The earliest evidence of toothbrushes like those we use today is from 1498, also from China. The bristles were made from hog hair.

Toothbrushes arrived in Europe in the 1600s but weren't commonly used until the 1900s.

The first nylon toothbrush was invented in 1938, but it was very hard. People didn't bother brushing much until the 1950s, when better toothbrushes had been developed.

Ancient cures for toothache you wouldn't want to try include strapping a toad to the jaw, picking bones out of wolf poo and wearing them, rubbing the ashes of burnt animal heads into the gums and washing the teeth in tortoise's blood three times a year.

Toothpaste **Form**

Once you have put this **Invention** to good use,
stick your Achieved Star here and fill in the form

Achieved

OPEN WIDE!

— TOOTH TRUTH —

You have probably had
one full set of teeth –
your 20 baby (or primary)
teeth – and are now
kitted out with your
permanent teeth. By the
time you reach 21, the
average amount of teeth
you'll have is 32, which
means in your lifetime
you'll have had an
average of 52 teeth!

Name of tooth 1

Name of tooth 2

Name of tooth 3

Name of tooth 4

Name of tooth 5

Name of tooth 6

Name of tooth 7

Name of tooth 8

UPPER

CHECK-UP

Can you match the teeth
to their names? Write your
answers in the boxes provided.
Answers at the back of the book.

a. First molar
b. Third molar (wisdom tooth)
c. Canine cuspid
d. Central incisor
e. Second molar
f. Lateral incisor
g. Second premolar / bicuspid
h. First premolar / bicuspid

CHECK-OUT

On the diagram, use different colours to
fill in the teeth that have had fillings, that
are missing, and that have had any dental
work to fix them.

COLOUR KEY

☐ Fillings   ☐ Fixed

☐ Missing / Haven't
appeared yet

LOWER

 At the same time you can check out these **Things You Wish You'd Invented:**
5: Fast Food • 18: Fizzy Drinks • 39: Toilets and Toilet Paper • 48: Aspirin
63: Anaesthetics • 85: Mirror • 91: Antibiotics • 95: Soap

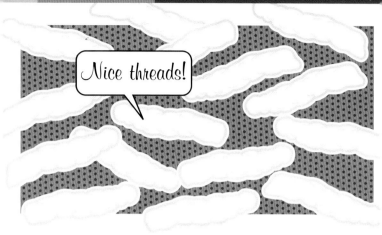

Silk

Silk is everyone's favourite luxury fabric, and has been for over 5,000 years, thanks to a humble moth ...

Mysterious Moths

No one really knows how or when silk was invented. The story goes that Lei Zu, an empress of China around 6,000 years ago, accidentally dropped the cocoon of a silkworm into her cup of tea. She saw that the cocoon quickly turned into long, smooth strands and decided to try spinning the strands into thread – as you would.

If you don't believe the legend, you'll have to guess how on earth someone found out that a particular moth's caterpillar, which eats only the leaves of the mulberry tree, makes a cocoon that produces fine fibres, and that these can be loosened in hot water and spun into silk. Someone in China had worked it out by around 3000 BC.

The Chinese kept the strange secret of silk-making for centuries, though silk was being exported from China by around 1000 BC. The ancient Romans paid high prices for silk, which they thought grew on trees. In the 1st century BC, the Chinese silk trade followed an established route, the silk road, all the way from China to the Mediterranean, with a second silk road going south to India. Around 200 BC, the silk secret was out: people found out about it in Korea and gradually the secret spread to the rest of the world.

 When it was first invented, the Chinese Emperor and his family were the only ones allowed to wear silk. Similarly, the Roman Emperor Tiberius tried to ban it, but it was just too popular. Silk was so valuable that for a while it was used as currency in China.

Silk **Form**

Once you have put this **Invention** to good use,
stick your Achieved Star here and fill in the form

Achieved

YOU WORM!

Although silkworms aren't actually worms, we shouldn't overlook how important the lowly worm is, in spite of looking completely useless. Test your knowledge with the quiz below. Once you've completed it, memorise the correct facts, then impress your friends to earn your star.

1. Which of the following is NOT a type of worm?

a) Horsehair worm
b) Leech
c) Fluke
d) Squareworm

2. How many earthworms can one acre of good soil contain?

a) Up to 100
b) Up to 1,000
c) Up to 500,000
d) Over a million

3. Which of the following statements is true?

a) Earthworms have no eyes
b) Earthworms have cold blood
c) Earthworms have no lungs
d) All of the above

4. How long was the largest earthworm ever found?

a) 6.5 cm
b) 65 cm
c) 6.5 m
d) 65 m

5. Why are earthworms so important?

a) Their excrement acts as a fertiliser, rich in nutrients
b) They play an important part in the food chain
c) They loosen the soil, allowing air and moisture to mix with it
d) All of the above

6. What happens if a worm is cut in half?

a) The tail end may grow a new head
b) The head end may grow a new tail
c) Two worms are created
d) The worm will die

7. Complete the following statement: All earthworms are ...

a) Male
b) Female
c) Neither male nor female
d) Both male and female

8. Where do most adult tapeworms live?

a) In the jungle
b) In fruit
c) In the intestines of animals and humans
d) In lakes

9. What do leeches eat to survive?

a) Blood
b) Soil
c) Water
d) Animal droppings

10. What is a computer worm?

a) Junk email
b) An internet connection
c) A computer virus
d) A self-replicating computer program

Answers at the
back of the book

At the same time you can check out these Things You Wish You'd Invented:
24: Hot-Air Balloon • 37: Fashion • 45: Jeans
50: Printing • 51: Make-up • 62: Bling • 85: Mirror

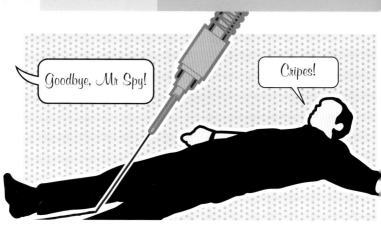

Laser

Lasers are useful for all sorts of things, including spectacular light shows –
no wonder there was a huge argument over who invented them.

Light Fantastic

Lasers produce a constant stream of photons (units of light) in a single
frequency, which means the light can be controlled and used in different
ways. Albert Einstein came up with the theory behind lasers in 1916, but it
wasn't put into practice for nearly 30 years ...

* In 1954 a group of scientists invented the 'maser' (microwave
  amplification by stimulated emission of radiation).
* The maser used microwaves. Research began into using light instead and
  the first device that produced laser light (light amplification by stimulated
  emission of radiation) was a ruby crystal, built in 1960 by physicist
  Theodore Harold Maiman, based on research by Charles Townes (who'd
  helped invent the maser) and Arthur Schawlow.
* Gordon Gould had also been researching laser technology and claimed to
  have invented the laser three years before Maiman's device. A big legal
  battle began, which Gould lost at first, but in 1977 he was granted several
  patents for his laser design. Still, Townes and Schawlow were awarded
  the Nobel Prize, which must have cheered them up a bit.
* Today, lasers read CDs and DVDs, cut metal, take measurements, make
  holograms and are used in surgery.

 Laser technology is being developed for use in warfare. The US and Israeli militaries
Tactical High Energy Laser has shot down targets in tests. They're not hand-held, *Star-Trek*-style devices, though – more like tanks for shooting down incoming missiles.

Laser **Form**

Once you have put this **Invention** to good use,
stick your Achieved Star here and fill in the form

Achieved

--- **LASER BRAIN** ---

Complete this laser quest to earn your star. Start at the top and follow each
laser beam down to discover some examples of the uses of laser technology.

ENTERTAINMENT:
CDs and DVDs
are read with
a laser

HEALTH:
Lasers can be
used in eye
surgery and types
of cosmetic surgery

WAR:
Powerful lasers
can be used in
warfare to shoot
down missiles

SHOPPING:
Lasers are
used in shops
to read barcodes

CONSTRUCTION:
Lasers are used
in construction to
cut out intricate
shapes

PRINTING:
Printers and
photocopiers
use laser
technology

SPACE:
Lasers have been
used to measure
how far the Moon is
from the Earth

 At the same time you can check out these **Things You Wish You'd Invented:**
8: Nuclear Weapons • 33: Battery • 35: CDs and DVDs • 40: Spectacles
44: Helicopter • 46: Music • 60: Inter-Stellar Travel • 70: Fireworks

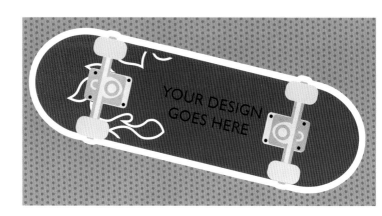

Skateboard

Is lipsliding or kickflipping your idea of a good time? If so, you must be glad someone invented the skateboard.

Sidewalk Surfing

Skateboards first appeared in California in the 1950s. No one's quite sure exactly when, or who first came up with the idea. Surfing (in the sea) was popular in the 1950s, so skateboarding became known as 'sidewalk surfing'. The first skateboards were home-made and might have evolved from 'crate scooters' – you can probably guess what they were. By the end of the 1950s skateboards were being manufactured and the sport became more and more popular.

For some reason, no one was very interested in skateboarding in the late 1960s but by the 1970s everyone was at it. New materials for wheels and boards improved performance and new moves were invented. Ramp skating developed after a California drought left swimming pools empty of water. In 1976 Alan Gelfand invented the 'aerial ollie' – lifting the board into the air by smacking the tail of the board on to the edge of a ramp with one foot and lifting up the front with the other.

More tricks were invented: now you can master the ollie kickflip, frontside and backside airs, and various types of grinds, including nose grinds, lipslides and 50-50 grinds.

Skateboarding was banned in Norway between 1978 and 1989 because the Norwegian government believed the sport was too dangerous. Now there are skateboarding bans in particular areas all over the world, but there's no complete nationwide ban anywhere.

Skateboard **Form**

Once you have put this **Invention** to good use,
stick your Achieved Star here and fill in the form

Achieved

BOARD, BOARD, BOARD

How are your skateboarding skills? Can you stay on a board for more than ten seconds? Can you do an ollie, tailside or a nosemanual? Do you even know what any of that means? Fill in the form below.

HIT THE DECK

Customise the top and bottom decks of your skateboard to make it individual and better looking than anyone else's!

If you don't own a skateboard, invent a design that wouldn't look out of place in a skate shop. Place a photograph or recreate the final design in the space provided below.

TOP

BOTTOM

TOP SKILLS

How do you rate your skateboarding skills?

Bad (as in bad)   50/50   Sweet!   Bad (as in good)   Awesome!

What is your signature trick?

WHICH OF THE FOLLOWING TYPES OF TRICK CAN YOU DO?

Ollie

Flip

Slide

Grind

Grab

Wheelie

List the injuries you've suffered because of skateboarding accidents ...

At the same time you can check out these Things You Wish You'd Invented:
15: Tattoo • 23: Plastic • 35: CDs and DVDs • 37: Fashion
41: Football • 45: Jeans • 46: Music • 75: Teenagers

Parachute

Have you ever felt like jumping out of a plane? Plenty of people have, but thankfully most of them did it after the invention of the parachute.

Skydiving

In fact parachutes were invented long before aeroplanes ...

- In 852 in Moorish Spain, Armen Firman jumped from a tall tower using a cloak on a wooden frame and lived to tell the tale.
- Leonardo da Vinci designed a parachute in the 1480s, though he didn't try it out. Croatian inventor Faust Vrančić jumped using a similar design in 1617.
- These early parachutes didn't catch on because there weren't any flying machines around to make them really useful. In 1783, around the same time as the first hot-air balloon (see **Invention** No. 24), Sebastien Lenormand invented a parachute, which he demonstrated by jumping from a tree – but it was only four metres high. A few years later, having refined his design, he successfully jumped from a tower.
- In 1785 Jean Pierre Blanchard used a dog to test his parachute design. The dog was fine, and so was Blanchard when he used the parachute in 1793 to escape a balloon accident.
- Up until then, parachute designs used a wooden frame. In 1797 André Jacques Garnerin jumped from a balloon over 900 m high using a frameless parachute much more like the modern-day kind, made of folded silk. Since then parachutes have saved thousands of lives. Some strange people even use them to jump out of planes for fun.

Cocking up: Robert Cocking was the first person to die in a parachute accident when the parachute he had designed himself failed to open in 1837. His fatal mistake was in forgetting to include the parachute's weight in his calculations.

Parachute **Form**

Once you have put this **Invention** to good use,
stick your Achieved Star here and fill in the form

Achieved

MAKE A PARACHUTE

The minimum age for doing a parachute jump is 16 in the UK (and then you still need written parental consent), so for the time being you'll just have to simulate a parachute jump by making your own parachute instead.

EQUIPMENT NEEDED

a large handkerchief (approximately 30 cm square), string, scissors, an action figure

WHAT TO DO

1. Tie a small knot in each corner of the handkerchief.

2. Cut four equal lengths of string (about 40 cm) and tie each bit of string to a corner of the handkerchief, above the knots.

3. Gather the loose ends of the strings together and tie them together in a knot.

4. Now you need to fasten on an action figure. Don't pick a really heavy action figure – you might need to experiment with different weights.

5. It's time to test your parachute. You may find that you need to drop the parachute from a greater height if it doesn't open properly the first time.

Did the parachute work first time? `y/n`

If not, what adjustments did you make?

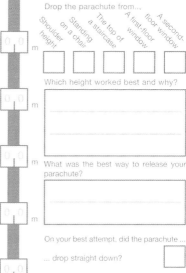

Try dropping your parachute from different heights to find out which produces the best result:

Drop the parachute from...

Shoulder height. | Standing on a chair | The top of a staircase | A first-floor window | A second-floor window

□ □ □ □ □

Which height worked best and why?

What was the best way to release your parachute?

On your best attempt, did the parachute ...

... drop straight down? □

... travel in the wind before landing? □

If it travelled, how far did it land from the drop site? `0,0` . `0,0` m

Did your action figure suffer any injuries? `y/n`

If yes, what happened?

`0,0` m

`0,0` m

`0,0` m

`0,0` m

`0,0` m

 At the same time you can check out these **Things You Wish You'd Invented**:
24: Hot-Air Balloon • 44: Helicopter • 69: Weather Machine
80: Silk • 93: Ejector Seat

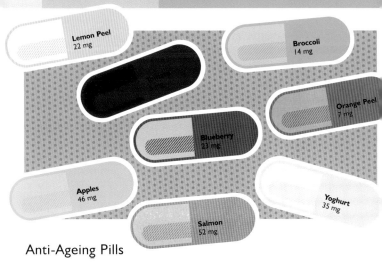

Lemon Peel
22 mg

Broccoli
14 mg

Orange Peel
7 mg

Blueberry
23 mg

Apples
46 mg

Yoghurt
35 mg

Salmon
52 mg

Anti-Ageing Pills

Instead of using make-up, special diets, strange remedies and cosmetic surgery, think how much simpler it would be if oldsters could just take a pill.

The Elixir of Life

Most of us would rather live for a lot longer than we're likely to, although the idea of living a long time but getting ever more decrepit is less appealing.

As we get older, cells in our bodies become damaged and we are more likely to suffer health problems. Eventually, of course, we suffer the biggest health problem of them all: death. Despite wild claims, none of the products available to buy today is capable of slowing down the ageing process. Scientists all over the world are busy looking for something that really works.

Researchers at the University of California at Berkeley have rejuvenated ageing rats by giving them two chemicals that affect their mitochondria – structures inside cells that are responsible for producing energy. Different research, also in California, has shown that restricting calories can make flies, worms and mice live longer. Instead of putting everyone on a very strict diet though, scientists are trying to mimic the effect using genetics.

But, for the time being, there's no miracle pill to stop people from ageing. Maybe we just need to change our attitude to old age – it would certainly be an awful lot easier.

Botulism is a dangerous type of food poisoning caused by the bacterium Clostridium botulinum. Doctors began using the bacterium to treat eye disorders and noticed it could paralyse muscles. Now people have it injected into their faces to smooth wrinkles!

Anti-Ageing Pills **Form**

Once you have put this **Invention** to good use,
stick your Achieved Star here and fill in the form

Achieved

ELIXIR OF LIFE

The elixir of life has been searched for time and time again over the centuries,
and although thousands of potions and lotions have been created, nothing has been
able to stop the ageing process. Some of the potions created in ancient China included
liquid metals, such as mercury and gold! Far from preventing ageing, the metals had the
opposite effect, and the poisonous elements in them accelerated death ... whoops!

YOU ARE WHAT YOU EAT

Over the last century, the life expectancy of the UK population has leapt to 76.6 years
for a male and 81 years for a female. In 1911 there were only 100 centenarians. Now
there are over 9,000! The reason we are all living longer is due to many factors, but can mainly
be put down to improvements in healthcare, nutrition and sanitation. And undoubtedly
things will continue to improve and advance in these areas. In fact, it is estimated
that by 2031 the UK will have almost 40,000 centenarians!

SUPER FOOD

Every now and again you'll hear about a new type of super food in the news. A super food is believed
to have greater health benefits than other foods. You'll be pleased to hear that chocolate is classed
as a super food BUT, as always, there's a catch. The benefits of chocolate are actually within the
cocoa content of the bar. You'll need to choose a dark chocolate bar with the highest cocoa content
to reap the benefits, and even then, you can only consume the chocolate in SMALL quantities!

Take a look at the list of super foods below. Tick the ones you've tried. Are there any you haven't had
before? If so, make a point of trying them all to find out which ones you like best, and persuade your
family to incorporate them into their daily diet – you can all stay young together!

☐ Alfalfa	☐ Flaxseeds	☐ Pomegranate
☐ Almonds	☐ Garlic	☐ Pumpkin (and pumpkin seeds)
☐ Apples	☐ Ginger	☐ Rice
☐ Avocados	☐ Kale	☐ Raspberries
☐ Bananas	☐ Leek	☐ Salmon
☐ Beans (various types)	☐ Lentils	☐ Sardines
☐ Beetroot	☐ Mackerel	☐ Soy
☐ Blueberries	☐ Nettle leaf	☐ Spinach
☐ Broccoli	☐ Oats	☐ Tea (especially green tea)
☐ Burdock root	☐ Olive oil	☐ Tomatoes
☐ Chilli peppers	☐ Onions	☐ Turkey
☐ Cocoa (dark chocolate)	☐ Oranges	☐ Walnuts
☐ Cranberries	☐ Parsley	☐ Whole grains (cereal, bread etc)
☐ Eggs	☐ Peel (orange and lemon)	☐ Yoghurt

At the same time you can check out these **Things You Wish You'd Invented:**
5: Fast Food • 48: Aspirin • 63: Anaesthetics • 66: Tea • 72: X-ray
77: Banana Suitcase • 91: Antibiotics • 100: Chindogu

I make you look goooooood!

Mirror

Before mirrors were invented you could always look at your lovely reflection by gazing into a still pool of water. But plucking your eyebrows must have been very tricky.

Through the Looking Glass

Humans seem to be obsessed with looking at their reflection – we're the only animal that does it as part of a daily routine, though chimps seem to enjoy it too. The earliest mirrors ever found were discovered in modern-day Turkey. They are made from obsidian, a volcanic glass that's naturally reflective, and are more than 7,000 years old.

Since then, people have made mirrors out of polished stones, metal and crystal. A glass hand-mirror was an ancient Roman fashion accessory. According to the Roman historian Pliny, the first glass mirrors were invented about 400 BC in Sidon in the Middle East. They were made by applying a very thin layer of gold, silver or copper to a sheet of glass. During the 19th century, processes were developed that enabled the glass surface to be coated with metal. Modern mirrors use a thin layer of aluminium on glass.

As well as the important purpose of admiring ourselves, mirrors also come in very handy for telescopes, microscopes and periscopes, seeing what's going on behind you when you're driving a car, and laughing at very fat and very skinny versions of yourself at fairgrounds.

Mirrors as weapons: Legend has it that the ancient mathematician and inventor Archimedes used large mirrors of polished bronze or copper to concentrate the Sun's rays and set fire to enemy ships.

Mirror **Form**

Once you have put this **Invention** to good use,
stick your Achieved Star here and fill in the form

Achieved

——— KALEIDOSCOPE ———

The word 'kaleidoscope' comes from the greek words 'beautiful', 'form' and 'view'. If you
make a kaleidoscope following the instructions below, you'll see why these words are so apt!

——— WHAT YOU NEED ———

3 rectangular mirrors of equal size, clear plastic, tracing paper, cardboard, scissors, Sellotape, coloured paper cut into tiny shapes (or confetti)

——— WHAT TO DO ———

1. Place your three mirrors side by side on a piece of cardboard, leaving a small gap between them.

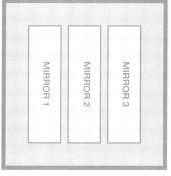

2. Glue the mirrors to the card and cut the cardboard down to size as shown.

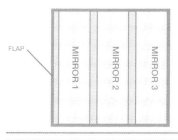

3. Bend the cardboard with mirrors over to form a long triangular tube and glue the flap down to make the structure rigid.

4. Make a triangular cover for the end of the kaleidoscope. Pierce a hole in the middle of the triangle. This is the eyehole.

5. Now cut out two triangles, one made of clear plastic and one of tracing paper. Both should be the same size as the end of your triangular tube. Sellotape two sides of your two triangles together to form a pouch. Pour some confetti or coloured paper into the pouch. Don't stuff it too full – the bits of paper should have room to move around inside.

6. Seal the third side of the triangular pouch with Sellotape so that the pieces of coloured paper can't fall out. Then use more Sellotape to fix the pouch to the open end of the tube, making sure the tracing paper side is facing out.

7. Point your kaleidoscope towards the light and look through the eyehole. You should see a pattern appear reflected in the mirrors, and if you turn your kaleidoscope the pattern will keep moving and changing.

At the same time you can check out these **Things You Wish You'd Invented**:
11: Fingerprinting • 13: Satellite • 30: Magic
37: Fashion • 51: Make-up • 59: Glass • 62: Bling

Tin-Opener

Most of us take this useful invention for granted now, but it would have been helpful if the tin-opener had been invented at the same time as the tin.

In-can-venient

Tinned food was invented by Peter Durand in 1810, and the first tinned food was produced in 1812. Unfortunately, no one had come up with a device for opening the tins. It was just as well that the first tins of food were used by the military – at least they had weapons handy for opening them. Instructions on the tins helpfully suggested using a hammer and chisel.

Tinned food went on sale to the public around 1830. For the next 25 years, people struggled with saws, chisels and other tools. Then, in 1855, Robert Yeates invented a sort of penknife including a special blade that could be used to open tins. Three years later, Ezra Warner of Connecticut, USA, patented a tin-opener shaped like a bent bayonet – but it was too dangerous for domestic use!

In 1870 William Lyman invented a tin-opener with a cutting wheel. It was a bit tricky to use, though – you had to try and make a hole in the centre of the can with one blade, then adjust the device to make the wheel cut around the edge. Improvements to Lyman's design were made in the 1920s and resulted in the modern rotary tin-openers still in use today. Electric tin-openers became available in the 1960s. The latest in tin-opening technology are devices that open tins without leaving sharp edges.

The first food tins were very heavy – some weighed half a kilo when empty. Durand's earliest cans were made of iron lined with tin and their sides were up to 5 mm thick. Tin-openers only came along when cans began to be made of thinner metal.

Tin-Opener **Form**

Once you have put this **Invention** to good use,
stick your Achieved Star here and fill in the form

Achieved

RE-RE-RE-USE

Recycling has become part of everyday life and hopefully, one day, everything will be recyclable!
For the time being, most of us can recycle our tin cans, food waste, glass and plastic (see
Invention No. 23) to help reduce emissions, save energy and cut production costs. Earning
your star for this form is simple: recycle your waste! Every little helps. For more info, visit
www.recyclenow.com, www.alupro.org.uk and **www.britglass.co.uk**, where you can
find fascinating facts about recycling, some of which have been listed below:

CAN YOU BELIEVE IT?

1 Recycling just ONE aluminium can saves enough energy to power a television for around three hours!

2 It only takes TWO HOURS for the UK population to produce enough waste to entirely fill the Royal Albert Hall!

3 If you recycled an aluminium can today, within SIX WEEKS you could be buying it off the shop shelf again!

4 If we recycled all the aluminium cans of drink the people of the UK buy every year, we'd need 14 million FEWER dustbins collected!

5 Recycling old aluminium is 95% MORE energy efficient than making brand-new aluminium!

GLASS ACT

6 Did you know that the energy saved from recycling ONE glass bottle will power a 100-watt light bulb for an hour? BUT ...

7 ... if you swap the 100-watt for a 60-watt bulb then that same bottle will power the 60-watt bulb for SIX hours instead!

8 AND that same recycled bottle could power your computer for 20 minutes or a washing machine for 10 minutes!

9 Creating new glass contributes 20% more to air pollution and 50% more to water pollution than recycling old glass.

10 On average, each person in the UK throws away the equivalent to their own body weight in rubbish every seven weeks.

TIN-CAN TELEPHONE

Another thing you can do with empty cans is to make a tin-can telephone. All you need is two
empty tin cans, a long piece of string, a parent with a hammer and a nail, and someone to talk too!

Firstly, check your empty cans. BE VERY CAREFUL – make sure there are no sharp edges on the cans as they can cause serious injuries. If there are, put the can back into the recycling and find another one.

Now you need a parent to hammer a nail into the middle of the base of the cans, to make a hole for the string.

When you have two holey cans,

thread the string through them and tie knots in the ends.

Congratulations! You've made a tin-can telephone!

Take one of the cans and get a friend to take the other. Make sure the string between you is pulled tight.

Now, speak into your can and your friend should listen by holding the other can to their

ear. They should hear you loud and clear! In this way you can conduct a conversation.

HOW IT WORKS

When the string is pulled tight between the cans and you begin to speak, the vibrations caused by your speech cause the string to vibrate. Those vibrations travel to your friend's can, which then amplifies your voice.

Passport

If you've had a new passport recently you'll have spent hours in photo booths trying to take a photo that meets complicated requirements and, at the same time, captures your unique beauty. But how long have passports been around?

Tickets, Passport, Toothbrush ...

In fact passports have been a requirement in most parts of the world for less than a hundred years. They existed before that but only for a few people in particular circumstances. Imagine, for example, that you're a courtier of Elizabeth I sent on an errand to Italy. You will probably be given a letter signed by the Queen that tells people who you are and asks that you are well treated while you're abroad – a passport. Tradespeople were sometimes given passports, allowing them to pass in and out of particular towns and cities. But most people didn't need passports until the First World War and could travel where they liked without them. Of course, not many people did a lot of travelling abroad in those days.

During the First World War, governments became very keen on identifying anyone passing in and out of their country, for obvious reasons, and made passports compulsory for everyone crossing the border in either direction. After the war, this rule remained. In 1920 the League of Nations agreed standards for passports for all its member countries, and most passports today are based on those standards: they identify the passport holder, ask for protection while abroad and give the holder the right to return.

Biometrics: If your passport was issued recently, it probably contains biometric information about you, for example, your fingerprints, distances between facial features, or the iris or retina in your eye. This information is stored in an electronic chip to improve security.

Passport **Form**

Once you have put this **Invention** to good use,
stick your Achieved Star here and fill in the form

Achieved

PLACES I'VE VISITED

Have you ever had your passport stamped? Passport stamps keep a colourful record of the
countries you've visited – although, these days, if you're a citizen of the European Union you
won't get stamped when you visit other EU countries. Why not keep a record here by filling in
the stamps below with all the countries you've been to – including those ones that didn't stamp
your passport! Tick the boxes if your parents had to apply for a visa before you made each trip.

 At the same time you can check out these **Things You Wish You'd Invented**:
7: Time Zones • 9: Money • 34: Teleporter • 52: Language
54: Steam Engine • 78: Language Decoder • 90: Maps

Computer

Imagine the world without computers. You'd have no internet to help you with your homework, and just think of all that post, photocopying and filing.

Making a Difference

The first computer was invented in 1834 – long before TV, telephones and even electricity. The inventor, Charles Babbage, called his computer the Difference Engine. It was essentially a calculator and since there was no electricity, it was mechanical. And very complicated. In fact he never quite managed to finish it. Babbage spent a further 37 years designing the Analytical Engine – a pre-cursor to the first working general-purpose computers.

Computers really got going in the 20th century:

- Konrad Zuse's Z3 was the first programmable computer, invented in 1941.
- The Colossus computer was the first completely electronic computer. It was used to crack German codes during the Second World War.
- By the end of the 1950s computers had become smaller and cheaper. (They were still about the size of a double-decker bus, though.)
- Microprocessors – programmable components measuring just a few millimetres – were invented by Intel employee Ted Hoff in 1971. Just one of them was as powerful as the huge 30-tonne computers of the 1940s.
- By the 1980s computers were small and cheap enough for individuals to buy and use at home. And today, computers are everywhere and most modern electronic devices, from washing machines to cars, contain one.

 Finished Engine: Although Charles Babbage never completed the Difference Engine himself, the Science Museum in London did manage to build one in 1991, to mark the 200th anniversary of Babbage's birth. And it worked!

Computer **Form**

Once you have put this **Invention** to good use,
stick your Achieved Star here and fill in the form

Achieved

--- **YOU'RE NOT THE BOSS OF ME** ---

Computers have taken over almost all aspects of our lives, from schoolwork and homework
to keeping in touch with your friends. But not so long ago computers didn't even exist.
Can you live without using one for at least a week? Sign the declaration below and see if
you have the will power to give it up.

I DECLARE: BY SIGNING THIS FORM I AGREE TO LIVE ONE WHOLE WEEK WITHOUT USING A COMPUTER AT ALL. HOWEVER TEMPTED I MAY BE, I VOW NOT TO TOUCH ONE.

MY COMPUTER IS NOT THE BOSS OF ME!

SIGNED:

--- **I HAVE THE WILL POWER!** ---

How did you do? Was the pull of your computer too much
or did your will power see you through? Write your results below.

How long did you stay
away from a computer?

I gave in within hours · I lasted a few days · I nearly did it but gave in at the end · I resisted for the whole week! · I'm still not using it!

How did you carry out the tasks you would
normally do on a computer?

How did you spend any freed-up time?

Would you do it again?

What is the best thing about having your
computer back?

At the same time you can check out these **Things You Wish You'd Invented:**
6: Photography • 13: Satellite • 35: CDs and DVDs • 49: Homework Machine
56: World Wide Web • 60: Inter-Stellar Travel • 81: Laser • 89: Barcodes

Barcodes

Have you ever thought about barcodes? Probably not, but they're absolutely everywhere, on just about everything you can buy. Before they were invented, someone had the thrilling job of sticking prices on everything, and an awful lot of counting went on in shops.

Clever Codes

Barcodes contain information – including price – that's readable by a scanning machine. They were invented by technology students Bernard Silver and Norman Woodland in 1949, although the system they came up with, using ink that glowed under ultraviolet light, wasn't the one we use today. First a working system had to be developed and a universal standard set. The barcode system we use was demonstrated for the first time by IBM in 1973. The following year the first ever purchase using a barcode was made, but barcode technology didn't become common until the 1980s. Now it's everywhere. As well as reading the price, barcode scanners can give information about how quickly things sell and can even re-order new stock.

It won't be long until barcodes are out of date and we're all remembering what a wearisome process shopping was before the invention of RFIDs. Radio frequency identification tags will soon mean that you can go shopping without having to queue up and pay at all. RFIDs, or smart labels, will be able to communicate with an electronic reader in your shopping trolley and send information to the shop, the manufacturer and your bank account.

 Historic gum: The first ever barcode purchase was of a 10-pack of Wrigley's Juicy Fruit chewing gum at a supermarket in Troy, Ohio. The chewy is now on display at the Smithsonian Institute's National Museum of American History in Washington DC.

Barcodes **Form**

Once you have put this **Invention** to good use,
stick your Achieved Star here and fill in the form

Achieved

— I AM NOT A NUMBER! —

Answer the following questions and make your own personal barcode. The chances of anyone
having the same barcode as you is incredibly remote as we are all different in so many ways.

Are you male or female? Put a '1' in Box A
if you're male and a '2' if you're female.

In which year were you born?
Put the last two digits of the year in Box B
and C. For example if you were born in
1995 put '9' in Box B and '5' in Box C.

Are you left- or right-handed?
Put a '3' in Box D if you're right-
handed, and a '4' if you're left-handed.

Do you have a birthmark? Put a '5' in
Box E if you do and a '6' if you don't.

What is your height in inches?
Put your answer in Box F and G.

What is your weight in kilograms?
Put your answer in Box H and I.

What colour are your eyes? In Box J put
'1' for amber, '2' for blue, '3' for brown, '4' for green,
'5' for grey, '6' for hazel, '7' for violet, '8' for other.

Now you have all your numbers, it's time to draw in
your barcode. Take a look at the barcode on the
opposite page. This is your barcode key and shows
you what patterns of lines you need to draw above
the numbers in your barcode below. Fill them in to
complete your unique barcode and use this design to
make badges, stickers or T-shirts tailor-made for you!

1 0 1 3 6 5 1

At the same time you can check out these **Things You Wish You'd Invented**:
5: Fast Food • 9: Money • 18: Fizzy Drinks • 27: Pizza • 33: Battery
35: CDs and DVDs • 37: Fashion • 46: Music • 71: Numbers • 88: Computer

Unfortunately, you are here

X

Pacific Ocean

Pacific Ocean

Dead
Man's Cove

Skull
Island

No Hope Island

Maps

Once people had worked out where everything is, which wasn't easy, the world started getting smaller and smaller ...

Mapping the World

- The first maps ever made were of the night sky – the Lascaux cave paintings (in modern-day France) show the positions of stars, and date from over 18,000 years ago. The oldest known land map dates from more than 4,000 years ago in ancient Mesopotamia (modern-day Iraq) – the clay tablet map shows a river valley.
- The ancient Greeks knew that the world was a sphere and were good map-makers. Ancient Greek Anaximader, who lived around 600 BC, was the first Greek to draw a map of the world, but it hasn't survived.
- Around AD 150 Greek astronomer Ptolemy drew a world map, showing the Mediterranean and parts of Africa and Asia. His map uses lines of latitude and longitude.
- In Europe, medieval maps were more symbolic than useful, showing Jerusalem as the centre of the world for religious reasons.
- The Age of Exploration, in the 1400s and 1500s, produced more and more accurate maps. In 1569 Gerard Mercator solved the problem of showing the spherical Earth on a two-dimensional map using clever calculations. We still use 'Mercator projection' today.
- Aerial photography in the 20th century made map-making more accurate than ever before.

Touchy-feely maps: Maps weren't always drawn on paper – 300 years ago the people of Greenland were carving maps out of wood. People used these 3-D maps to navigate the coast by touching them rather than looking at them.

Maps **Form**

Once you have put this **Invention** to good use,
stick your Achieved Star here and fill in the form

Achieved

WISH YOU WERE HERE

With computer mapping programs you can find aerial photographs taken by satellites of almost
anywhere in the world. And the best thing is, with just a few clicks of a button and a little help
from everyone's favourite toy, the internet, you can look at these amazing images for free!
See if you can find an aerial view of your house. Print it out and place it below. If you
can't find your house, pick a place you wish you could be in.

X
I AM
HERE

At the same time you can check out these Things You Wish You'd Invented:
7: Time Zones • 13: Satellite • 24: Hot-Air Balloon • 26: Submarine • 34: Teleporter
44: Helicopter • 60: Inter-Stellar Travel • 87: Passport • 88: Computer

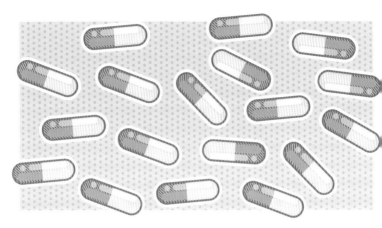

Antibiotics

Far fewer people die from infections now than fifty years ago. One of the main reasons is an amazing discovery ...

Old Mould

Antibiotics are used as a medicine to fight bacteria – you might have taken them if you've had an infection. Today we use antibiotics that are manufactured in labs, but they were originally discovered as natural substances. Penicillin was the first to be discovered, quite by accident ...

Alexander Fleming was a doctor with a messy lab. He'd been growing bacteria in Petri dishes and left a pile of them waiting to be cleaned. Fleming noticed that one of them had mould growing on it that seemed to have killed the bacteria in the dish, and decided to examine it more closely. The mould was penicillium and Fleming managed to isolate the bacteria-killing chemicals it produced, which are now known as penicillins.

Fleming made his discovery in the 1920s but no one took much notice of it until the Second World War, when chemists Howard Florey and Ernst Chain carried on his work and came up with a purified form of penicillin. The medicine began to be mass produced for the first time, and went on to save millions of lives. Fleming, Florey and Chain shared the Nobel Prize for Medicine in 1945. Today, penicillin-based antibiotics are still the safest and most commonly prescribed.

 Alexander Fleming had noticed that bacteria developed resistance to antibiotics if the medicine wasn't taken for long enough or in too low a dose. Just four years after drug companies began mass producing penicillin, microbes began appearing that could resist it.

Antibiotics **Form**

Once you have put this **Invention** to good use,
stick your Achieved Star here and fill in the form

Achieved

I TOLD YOU I WAS ILL

Think back to the last time you felt really ill. Was it an infection of some
kind? Did you have to take antibiotics? Fill in this form. Start by ticking
the relevant boxes below to record your symptoms.

Blocked nose · Headache · Sore throat · Nausea · Earache · Stomach ache · Toothache · Constip- ation · Diarrhoea · Temp- erature · Spots · Rash

☐ ☐ ☐ ☐ ☐ ☐ ☐ ☐ ☐ ☐ ☐ ☐

Cough · Aching all over · Shivering · Vomiting · Swollen glands · Other

☐ ☐ ☐ ☐ ☐ ☐

If other, please specify

What was the diagnosis?

Did you see a doctor? ☐ y/n

What medicines (if any) did you have to take?

Did they work? ☐ y/n   How quickly did
you get better?

☐.☐ days   ☐.☐ weeks   ☐.☐ months

Rate the seriousness of your illness

☆ ☆ ☆ ☆ ☆
Bad · Pretty bad · Awful · Terrible · At death's door

How did you spend most
of your convalescence?

TV · Radio · Read- ing · Just feel- ing bad · Computer games · Sleeping

☐ ☐ ☐ ☐ ☐ ☐

Rate the effectiveness of your medication

☆ ☆ ☆ ☆ ☆
No effect · Poor · OK · Good · Excellent

At the same time you can check out these **Things You Wish You'd Invented:**
4: Cloning • 20: Thermometer • 39: Toilets and Toilet Paper • 40: Spectacles
48: Aspirin • 63: Anaesthetics • 73: Sunscreen • 79: Toothpaste • 95: Soap

Vinyl Records

If you wanted to listen to music before the 1870s, your only option was to go to a public performance or listen to friends, family or worse still yourself playing or singing. People must have suffered centuries of bad music in this wa

World Records

The famous inventor Thomas Edison invented the phonograph in 1877, which made the first ever sound recordings on foil cylinders. Edison didn't foresee a future where people listened to the best music in the world using his invention – he thought it would be used as a dictation machine in offices, which is much less entertaining.

Edison's foil cylinders were soon replaced by wax ones, and only ten years after his invention the cylinders were replaced by flat discs, invented by Emil Berliner in 1887. These discs were much easier to mass produce than cylinders. At first they were made from a brittle substance containing shellac, a substance made from beetle poo, but by 1930 the first vinyl plastic discs were sold, which were much more difficult to break and less horrible to think about. The first flat discs were initally used in toys, but by the mid-1890s Berliner had set up a gramophone company which sold the discs and the gramophones to play them on.

These plastic discs, known as records, continued to be used until the 1980s, when everyone began to buy CDs instead. They're still used by DJs and very old-fashioned people.

 Thomas Edison famously said, 'Genius is one per cent inspiration, ninety-nine per cent perspiration.' He must have perspired a lot as he filed more than a thousand patents in his lifetime. His voice was the first sound to be recorded on his phonograph. His words were: 'Mary had a little lamb.'

Vinyl Records **Form**

Once you have put this **Invention** to good use,
stick your Achieved Star here and fill in the form

Achieved

MUSIC TO YOUR EARS

Riffle through your parents' record collection and pick out records you don't think you've heard before. How have they stood the test of time? Listen – with an open mind! – and review each of the records in turn, making a note of your thoughts below to earn your star.

Star ratings: 1 – Embarrassing! • 2 – Not my cup of tea • 3 – OK • 4 – Pretty good! • 5 – Awesome!

At the same time you can check out these **Things You Wish You'd Invented**:
10: Time Machine • 21: Guitar • 23: Plastic • 25: Poetry
35: CDs and DVDs • 37: Fashion • 46: Music • 67: Dancing • 75: Teenagers

Ejector Seat

Although it looks funny in action, the ejector seat has saved thousands of lives since its invention in the middle of the 20th century.

Supersonic Seats

An ejector seat is designed to catapult the pilot and crew out of a plane in an emergency, inflate a parachute once the seat is clear of the aircraft, and bring them safely to land. Before ejector seats were invented there were parachutes (see **Invention** No. 83) but the crew would have to try and jump clear of the aircraft first ... which can be a bit tricky when a plane's plummeting to earth at hundreds of kilometres per hour.

The Second World War created an obvious need for this invention. The first ejector seat was pioneered by the German company Heinkel in 1940, and the Swedish company SAAB developed its own ejector seat independently the following year. Both used compressed air to shoot the seats out of the aircraft. In 1942 one of the German test pilots became the first person to escape from a plane using an ejector seat in an emergency.

After the war, some planes became so fast that it was impossible to escape from them using just a parachute. After the early compressed-air ejector seats, explosive charges were used to power the seats. And from the 1960s, rocket-powered ejector seats were made for use at supersonic speeds. A few pilots have ejected at speeds over 1,300 km/h!

By the seat of your pants: Ejector seats save thousands of lives but they are designed for use in dire emergencies only. The seats shoot out of the plane with such force that they can cause serious, sometimes career-ending injuries.

Ejector Seat **Form**

Once you have put this **Invention** to good use,
stick your Achieved Star here and fill in the form

Achieved

--- **TYPES OF AVIATION** ---

In fewer than seventy years the history of aviation went from nothing to putting a man on the Moon. Take a look at the types of aviation below: which have you flown in or seen? Hopefully you'll never have to use the ejector seat in any of these!

Out of all the aircraft it is possible to travel in, you'll probably have travelled most in a jumbo jet. How many flights in a jumbo jet have you made?

Have you ever flown in this type of flying vehicle? After a jumbo jet, the vehicles in this group are the easiest to hitch a ride in.

☐ Glider   ☐ Micro-light   ☐ Hang-glider

☐ Heli-copter   ☐ Light aircraft   ☐ Hot-air balloon

It's doubtful that you'll ever get to fly in any of the following aircraft, but have you seen them in action?

☐ Antique plane   ☐ Military helicopter   ☐ Military aircraft

☐ Airship   ☐ Super-sonic jet   ☐ Space travel

On the map below, draw any long-distance flights you've made around the world

At the same time you can check out these **Things You Wish You'd Invented**:
10: Time Machine • 24: Hot-Air Balloon • 34: Teleporter • 44: Helicopter
60: Inter-Stellar Travel • 83: Parachute • 100: Chindogu

Flip Flops

Love them or hate them, flip flops have become an icon of summer fashion ...

Sandals and Jandals

Some experts believe that our ancestors were wearing sturdy shoes between 40,000 and 26,000 years ago. No one's found any shoes from that long ago, though. The evidence has to do with our toes, which became smaller and less useful around that time. Apparently, if you don't wear strong shoes, you need to use your toes much more to balance. So if we carry on wearing flip flops, which don't help us to balance, perhaps we'll evolve stronger toes again. In fact, flip flops are criticised because wearers' toes have to grip in a way that can damage feet.

No one knows when they were invented, but flip flops are thought to be based on traditional Japanese sandals called *zori*. The main difference is that modern flip flops are made of rubber, while zori traditionally have a wooden sole and use plant fibres for the 'thong' part. In some areas of the world flip flops are known as 'jandals' – short for Japanese sandals.

Flip flops are cheap to make, comfy, hard-wearing and perfect for the beach, and they've become more popular than ever in recent years. As well as the ordinary, cheap, rubber kind, now you can make a fashion statement with expensive designer flip flops. There are even flip flops that cost *thousands* of pounds: a gold-and-diamond-encrusted pair.

Prehistoric shoe fetish: The oldest footwear ever found are 9,000-year-old sandals made of bark and sagebrush plant fibres. Seventy pairs of the skillfully woven sandals were discovered in a cave in Oregon, USA, in 1938.

Flip Flops **Form**

Once you have put this **Invention** to good use,
stick your Achieved Star here and fill in the form

Achieved

FLIPPING FLOPS

Customise the flip flops below, then create the design on an actual pair of flip flops to
earn your star. You could attach fake flowers, stickers or sequins to the thongs to liven
them up, and paint the soles. Experiment with different fabrics and materials, but be
careful not to make your flip flops uncomfortable or dangerous to wear, unless you
simply intend to have them on show as a piece of artwork!

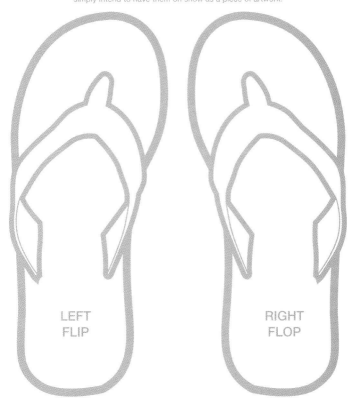

LEFT
FLIP

RIGHT
FLOP

 At the same time you can check out these Things You Wish You'd Invented:
23: Plastic • 37: Fashion • 40: Spectacles • 45: Jeans • 62: Bling • 73: Sunscreen

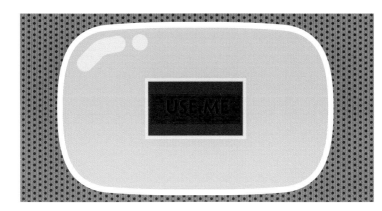

Soap

The world would be a far less fragrant place without soap, and what would we buy Grandma for her birthday?

Come Clean

It's anybody's guess how people washed in the distant past. Maybe they didn't bother and just picked off the crusty bits. Soap is an unlikely combination of fat and any alkaline substance, so it's amazing that anyone invented it at all.

- The ancient Mesopotamians somehow worked out that mixing animal fat with wood ash makes a substance that can clean clothes and people. They made soap in clay cylinders as far back as 2800 BC.
- The ancient Egyptians were using soap made from fats and alkaline salts by about 1500 BC. Maybe they found out about it from their neighbours, the Mesopotamians.
- The ancient Romans were very fond of bathing and built public baths all over their empire, but they didn't use soap. There's some evidence to suggest that Roman women used a soap-like substance on their hair starting from around AD 50.
- People were making soap in Europe by the 600s, but they weren't using it nearly enough. The Middle Ages saw personal hygiene at its lowest point. Soap was a luxury item until the middle of the 19th century, so be very glad you weren't around in those days.

Getting into scrapes: Instead of using soap the ancient Romans cleaned themselves by oiling their bodies, then scraping off the oil using a special scraper called a 'strigil'. Really posh Romans would have a slave do the scraping for them.

Soap **Form**

Once you have put this **Invention** to good use,
stick your Achieved Star here and fill in the form

Achieved

SLIPPERY CUSTOMERS

If you're fed up of smelling of roses, make your own soap and you can smell however you like!

EQUIPMENT NEEDED

a neutral glycerin soap bar (available from health or craft shops), a knife, a wooden spoon, a microwaveable bowl, a microwave, various food colourings, essential oils, moulds (you can improvise with washed-out food or drink containers – or buy proper soap moulds from a craft shop).

BASIC SOAP

1. Cut the soap into small chunks or grate into thin shavings. Be careful not to cut yourself!

2. Put the soap into a microwaveable bowl and heat in a microwave until it has melted (about 50 seconds) or you can melt it in a saucepan on a cooker.

3. If you'd like to add colour, add it now drop by drop, stirring with a wooden spoon, until your soap is the colour you want. You can also add a scent at this point, mixing a few drops of the essential oil of your choice.

4. Pour the liquid soap into your mould. The soap will take about 45 minutes to harden, depending on the size of it.

STRIPY SOAP

To create stripes of colour in your soap, follow basic steps 1–3, but then rather than pouring all the colour into one mould, divide it into four moulds. You will end up with a shallow layer of colour at the bottom of each. Now you need to repeat this process using a different colour each time until you have built up four stripy soaps.

Try to add each new layer of coloured soap while the previous layer is still a bit soft. When all your layers are in place, leave it to harden fully.

SWIRLY SOAP

To create swirls of colour in your soap, follow basic steps 1–4 but don't add any colouring to the soap until it is poured into the mould.

When the soap is in its mould, add a few drops of one colour at one end, and a different colour at the other end (add other colours too, if you want). When you've added your drops of colour, take a toothpick or spoon and use it to stir the colours into the soap and create swirls. Leave to harden.

CHUNKY SOAP

To create chunks of colour in your soap, you need first of all to cut up a coloured soap (home-made or bought) into little chunks and put these chunks into the bottom of your mould.

Then make a different coloured soap, following basic steps 1–4, pouring the liquid soap into the mould over the chunks. Leave to harden.

(You can insert other things into the soap bar, such as a plastic spider to scare your mum!)

At the same time you can check out these **Things You Wish You'd Invented:**
11: Fingerprinting • 39: Toilets and Toilet Paper • 48: Aspirin
63: Anaesthetics • 79: Toothpaste • 91: Antibiotics

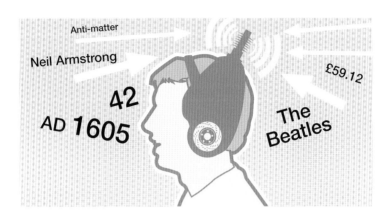

Know-It-All Hat

If you had the answer to every question ever asked, then you'd win every quiz and competition you ever took part in. But to have this knowledge without a know-it-all device, your brain would have to hold all the information that exists everywhere ever – in the dictionary, encyclopaedia, *Guinness Book of World Records*, and pretty much *every* book *ever* written in *every single language*! That's a lot of information.

I Know Something You Don't Know!

Your hat would have to be a sophisticated computer that could transmit information directly to the wearer's brain. It would also need to be able to detect when you were being asked a question, so it could self-activate its search for the answer. The information could be collected in a similar way to how the internet works, but it would have to be able to search through all that information in a much faster and more intelligent fashion.

To solve the problem of how to hold the vast quantity of data required, your hat could work in conjunction with other hats, each holding a limited amount of information, and connect wirelessly with the hat network to find the required answer. Once located, the answer could be 'beamed' back to your hat in seconds, and you would hear the answer in your head. All you'd have to do is repeat the answer out loud (acting as if you've only just remembered it to cover any short delay!). It would bring a new meaning to the phrase 'keep it under your hat'!

Norris Macwhirter probably wouldn't have needed a know-it-all hat. Co-founder of *The Guinness Book of World Records*, Norris had a photographic memory and could recite any answer in the book from memory. Mozart is also thought to have had a photographic memory.

Know-It-All Hat **Form**

Once you have put this **Invention** to good use,
stick your Achieved Star here and fill in the form

Achieved

--------- **I KNOW EVERYTHING!** ---------

So you've nearly finished reading this book and you reckon you pretty much know it all already ...
well, not quite yet. There's plenty more to learn about the inventions in this book, and you can start
by doing this quiz, which will reveal some rather interesting and unexpected extra facts. Memorise
the answers and impress your friends with the incredible (but quite pointless facts) to earn your star.

1. INTER-STELLAR TRAVEL: What was the name of the first animal in space and what was it?

2. PLAYING CARDS: What was different about the playing cards sent as gifts to US prisoners in the Second World War?

3. TIME: How long is a Martian year?

4. FAST FOOD: By what name was Michel Lotito, the man who ate an entire aeroplane, also known by?

5. PRISON: What job did notorious gangster Al Capone's business card claim he did?

6. EJECTOR SEAT: What colour is an aeroplane's black box recorder?

7. LANGUAGE: What does 'kangaroo' mean?

8. CLONING: In the 16th century, Dutch carrot farmers decided to breed orange carrots. What colour were they before then?

9. GUNPOWDER: Why is a tank called a tank?

10. X-RAY: You begin life with 300 bones but as you grow up the number changes. How many does the average adult have?

11. CONCRETE: Which bone in the human body is stronger than concrete?

12. ANTIBIOTICS: Do you transfer more germs to another person by shaking hands or by kissing?

13. TOOTHPASTE: What can't teeth do that all other parts of the human body can?

14. PIZZA: How long did it take Tom Waes to eat a 12" pizza on 2 December 2006?

15. TEA: How many people were involved in the world's biggest tea party in Nishio, Japan, on 8 October 2006?

At the same time you can check out these **Things You Wish You'd Invented**:
4: Cloning • 9: Money • 10: Time Machine • 56: World Wide Web
60: Inter-Stellar Travel • 78: Language Decoder • 88: Computer • 100: Chindogu

Alcoholic Drinks

Alcoholic drinks are made when the sugars found in plants are left to go off. A very, very long time ago, people discovered that grains of barley, wheat and corn, different types of fruit, and even honey, could be fermented to produce a drink that did more than quench your thirst – and it could play a role in hygiene, medicine, nutrition and religion too. It was probably discovered by accident, but we don't know when or how.

Ancient Alcohol

In various ancient cultures, alcohol was used in religious rites – perhaps its effects were thought to be supernatural. Many ancient societies worshipped gods of wine or beer. It wasn't limited to the priests, though, and there are various references to people staggering about drunk and warnings of the need for moderation in ancient Egyptian and Mesopotamian records.

The oldest wine ever found was discovered in a Stone Age pottery jar in the mountains of modern-day Iran. Amazingly, residues of the liquid had survived more than 7,000 years to be identified by scientists as a wine that was probably a bit like the Greek drink retsina. Another Neolithic site in Iran contained tiny amounts of a substance that experts think is beer. It's 6,000 years old. And the ancient Egyptians were brewing beer at least 4,500 years ago. Today, beer is the bestselling alcoholic drink. More than 133 billion litres are sold every year around the world – that's over 20 litres per person!

Drunk as a monk: Champagne, the poshest alcoholic tipple, was invented by a monk called Dom Pierre Perignon. He spent years trying to remove the bubbles from the wine he had made, before realising that people seemed to like them!

Alcoholic Drinks **Form**

Once you have put this **Invention** to good use,
stick your Achieved Star here and fill in the form

Achieved

DRUNK AS A SKUNK

Test your knowledge with the quiz below. Once you've completed it, memorise the
correct facts, then impress your friends to earn your star. Answers at the back of the book.

1. On average, how long does it take the
   body to process one unit of alcohol?

a) 10 mins
b) 1 hour
c) 3 hours
d) 4 hours

2. Which of the following theories are
   thought to be the reason why,
   historically, people clink glasses?

a) The drinks splashed over into each
   other, ensuring that if there was poison
   in one of the glasses, everyone had to
   drink it
b) Stretching out the arm to clink glasses
   made people's coats lift to reveal that
   they did not have a weapon on them
c) The clinking noise made by the glass
   was to ward off evil spirits
d) All of the above

3. Which of the following alcoholic drinks
   is also a word in the aviation alphabet
   (known as the **NATO phonetic
   alphabet**)?

a) Beer
b) Gin
c) Vodka
d) Whiskey

4. What can alcohol do to the body?

a) Give you spots
b) Give you bad breath
c) Make you put on weight
d) Make you sick
e) All of the above

5. Which organ in your body has the job
   of breaking down alcohol?

a) Heart
b) Liver
c) Kidney
d) Stomach

6. National Prohibition – the banning of
   alcohol in the USA – started in 1920
   and lasted ...

a) 3 months
b) 3 years
c) 13 years
d) 30 years

7. Who said: 'I may be drunk, Miss,
   but in the morning I will be sober
   and you will still be ugly'?

a) George W. Bush
b) Ernest Hemingway
c) Winston Churchill
d) Lord Byron

8. What is 'Drunken Fist'?

a) A card game
b) A battle cry
c) A martial art
d) A term to describe someone who
   is too drunk to hold their glass

9. What did the Vikings use as
   drinking vessels?

a) Helmets
b) Skulls
c) Shoes
d) Flower pots

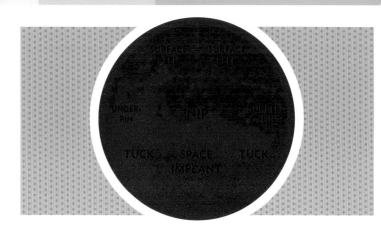

Terraforming

If we carry on ruining the planet it won't be long before the world is uninhabitable. Or it might become too crowded. Either way, it's always a good idea to have a Plan B.

Brave New World

Terraforming transforms another planet so that it ends up similar to Earth and humans can live there. The idea's simple, but putting it into practice isn't ...

- First, choose your planet. Mars is a popular option since it's so near. If you set foot there now, you'd be frozen and/or gassed in an instant, but Mars does have some elements that could sustain life and it's quite similar to the Earth billions of years ago.
- The temperature has to be right for humans to live without freezing or boiling. One suggested way of doing this is to set up vast mirrors to reflect the heat of the Sun.
- You don't want everyone to have to carry huge tanks of breathable air wherever they go, so you need the right atmosphere. 'Paraterraforming' would be one way of doing this: simply make an enormous enclosure with a transparent roof a kilometre or two above the planet's surface, then anchor it and pressurise it with breathable air. Hey presto.

That's just the start – you'd also need sources of water and food. As you can see, terraforming is tricky and requires a lot of technology that doesn't yet exist. But you never know, maybe you'll be able to retire to Mars.

More Martian statistics: The atmosphere of Mars is mostly carbon dioxide and the average temperature is -62°C. A big draw for tourists is the biggest volcano in the solar system: Olympus Mons is 27 km high and 550 km wide.

Terraforming **Form**

Once you have put this **Invention** to good use,
stick your Achieved Star here and fill in the form

Achieved

SPACE RACE

By 2020 there will be a base on the Moon. This will be the first time human beings have lived on
any celestial body other than Earth. But the Moon isn't ideal for terraforming, unlike Mars, which
has similar properties to Earth. Try to imagine what the Moon and Mars will look like when humans
start to populate them – after all, it's possible you might be around to witness both these events!

FULL MOON
What do you believe the moon base in 2020
will look like? Draw it on the diagram below

LIFE ON MARS
After Mars has been terraformed, what do
you think it will look like? Draw your vision
on the diagram below

TERRAFORM YOUR ROOM

If you could terraform your bedroom, what would it be like? Draw your new room in the space provided

 At the same time you can check out these Things You Wish You'd Invented:
4: Cloning • 6: Photography • 8: Nuclear Weapons • 9: Money • 10: Time Machine
13: Satellite • 34: Teleporter • 60: Inter-Stellar Travel • 69: Weather Machine

Sticky Tape and Blu-tack

Wrapping gifts and putting up posters and decorations would be pretty hard without these simple inventions.

A Sticky Situation

The first sticky tape was invented in 1925 by Richard Drew, an engineer at the company 3M. Drew had noticed that the fashion for painting cars in two colours was causing problems for the spray-painters. So he came up with an adhesive tape that could mask part of the car, then be removed, making a very neat join between the two different colours. In 1930 Drew came up with the first transparent sticky tape, known as Scotch tape in the USA. In the UK the Sellotape Company began producing sticky tape in 1937.

How Tacky

Generations of teenagers have stuck posters to their bedroom walls thanks to a 1971 invention, Blu-tack. Unlike sticky tape, it won't tear off the wallpaper and you can reuse it. It was discovered by accident during the development of a heavy-duty glue by the US adhesive company Bostick.

> **Glue**
>
> Thousands of years ago the first adhesives were made from tree resin.
>
> Glue made from animal skins dates back to Egyptian times.
>
> In the 1700s the first ever glue factory opened in Holland. The glue was still being made from animal skins.
>
> In the 1750s glue made from fish was invented – which must have been rather smelly.
>
> From the beginning of the 20th century adhesives began to be made from plastics.

The latest sticky invention is a glue that bonds surfaces together even though it's only one nanometre thick (one *thousandth of a millionth* of a metre). It bonds at high temperatures and could be used for gluing microscopic components and computer chips.

Sticky Tape and Blu-tack **Form**

Once you have put this **Invention** to good use,
stick your Achieved Star here and fill in the form

Achieved

STICKY ART

You know the obvious uses for sticky tape and Blu-tack, but have you ever thought about using these clever materials to make pieces of art? Some celebrated artworks are made of stranger materials than these. For example, the artist Chris Ofili won the £20,000 Turner Prize in 1998 for his artwork made partly of elephant dung!

STICKY TAPE ART

Name of piece

Art critics can get carried away with their insights into the art they review. Take the opportunity to say something profound about your 'work of art' here

Place a photograph of your work of art here

BLU-TACK ART

Name of piece

Art critics can get carried away with their insights into the art they review. Take the opportunity to say something profound about your 'work of art' here

Place a photograph of your work of art here

At the same time you can check out these **Things You Wish You'd Invented:**
6: Photography • 9: Money • 16: Pencils • 23: Plastic
29: Post-It Notes • 42: School • 100: Chindogu

Chindogu

Chindogu isn't the name of an actual invention – it's the Japanese name for the creation of pointless inventions that work but aren't practical. The word *chindogu* translates as 'useless tool'.

Heath Robinson Design*

Imagine a device designed to grab toast as it pops out of a toaster – one that used a mechanical hand attached to a powerful spring to catch the bread in mid-flight. This would require complex engineering to carry out what is an unnecessary task. If flying toast was a problem, the easier option would be to loosen the spring on the toaster or simply to buy a new toaster.

Some chindogu inventions, such as an umbrella that can shield you from rain from head to toe, would certainly get you noticed – but not for the right reasons, that is if you ever dared use it in public.

An easy chindogu invention to get you started would be a long stick designed to push the buttons on your TV. Who needs remote controls?

Some Ideas That Didn't Catch On ...
(if they had they wouldn't be chindogu!)

Portable zebra crossing
Roll it out like a mat and cross roads anywhere!

Butterstick
Like a glue stick but used to apply butter to toast

Duster slippers for cats
Your cats clean your floors as they walk around!

Chin stand
Catch 40 winks while you travel on public transport – without falling over

Solar-powered torch
Great idea in principle, but it can't work in the dark!

---

*'Heath Robinson' is a term used to describe any ingenious but ridiculous and complicated contraption, and is named after the English cartoonist W. Heath Robinson (1872–1944), who is best remembered for his delightful depictions of eccentric inventions.

Chindogu **Form**

Once you have put this **Invention** to good use,
stick your Achieved Star here and fill in the form

Achieved

MY GREAT IDEAS

In the space below create your own chindogu invention. It can be as
daft as you like. In fact, the more pointless and crazy the idea, the better!

At the same time you can check out these **Things You Wish You'd Invented:**
49: Homework Machine • 55: Duplication Machine • 60: Inter-Stellar Travel
69: Weather Machine • 77: Banana Suitcase • 96: Know-It-All Hat

Room 101

Finally, **Invention** No. 101 has to be Room 101. If only there was a place you could banish all those inventions you wish had never been invented in the first place, some of which may already have been mentioned in this book ...

The Room 101 idea first appeared in the book *Nineteen Eighty-Four*, written by George Orwell. It is a torture chamber where prisoners are confronted by their own worst nightmares. The main character, Winston Smith, is taken to Room 101 and comes face to face with his deepest fear – rats.

Inventions Room 101

Which inventions would you cast into Room 101? Open the door and throw in all those pointless machines that waste your time and ruin your day, or, worst still, pose a threat to life or the environment. Here are some suggestions:

- **Electric hand dryers**. These inventions never work properly! You either have to fight to keep the air flow going and risk burning your hands, or give up and dry your hands on the back of your jeans! Banish them!
- **School**. The institution we love to hate. Would you banish the whole thing or just certain classes and teachers, or just the homework?
- **Clowns**. Some people love clowns but others find them more scary than spiders! Would you send in the clowns?
- **Mobile phones**. Some say one of the most annoying things ever invented! Would you give yours up?

Banished by guests on the TV show, *Room 101*: cheese (Paul Daniels), caravans (Jeremy Clarkson), instruction manuals (Phil Collins), clipboards (Ross Noble), the piece of cotton that holds new pairs of socks together (Michael Parkinson) and Room 101 (Stephen Fry).

Room 101 **Form**

Once you have put this **Invention** to good use,
stick your Achieved Star here and fill in the form

Achieved

ROOM 101 HATED INVENTIONS

List your three most hated inventions and why you want to get rid of them.

INVENTION 1

Why do you hate this invention? Why would the world be a better place without it?

INVENTION 2

Why do you hate this invention? Why would the world be a better place without it?

INVENTION 3

Why do you hate this invention? Why would the world be a better place without it?

At the same time you can check out these **Things You Wish You'd Invented:**
2: Mobile Phone • 4: Cloning • 5: Fast Food • 8: Nuclear Weapons • 9: Money
12: Dynamite • 37: Fashion • 42: School • 75: Teenagers • 88: Computer

Answers

Answers Page

Hey! No cheating!

INVENTION NO. 2
MOBILE PHONE: TXT TST

KOTL = Kiss on the lips
LOL = Laughing out loud
SOHF = Sense of humour failure
EOD = End of discussion
FYEO = For your eyes only
GAL = Get a life
KISS = Keep it simple, stupid
PTB = Please text back
2L8 = Too late!
T+ = Think positive

MOBILE PHONE: EMOTICONS

----<--(@ = A rose
d-_-b = Someone with headphones on
~~~>_<~~~ = Crying uncontrollably

INVENTION NO. 3
MATCHES: HAVE YOU MET YOUR MATCH?

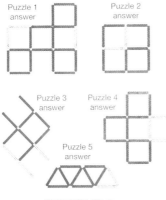

Puzzle 1 answer

Puzzle 2 answer

Puzzle 3 answer

Puzzle 4 answer

Puzzle 5 answer

INVENTION NO. 8
NUCLEAR WEAPONS: NEW CLEAR ANSWERS

1. b / 2. c / 3. b. / 4. b / 5. d
6. b / 7. c / 8. b / 9. d

INVENTION NO. 12
DYNAMITE: WANTED: DEAD OR ALIVE

<u>Ned Kelly</u> • Edward Kelly • Bushranger • Dan Kelly • Tried to escape in a suit of armour and failed • Hanged

<u>Billy the Kid</u> • Henry McCarty • Feuding gunfighter • Jesse Evans • Killed 21 men, one for each year of his life • Shot by Sheriff Pat Garrett

<u>Butch Cassidy</u> • Robert LeRoy Parker • Train and bank robber • Sundance Kid • Formed a gang known as the 'Wild Bunch' • Uncertain

<u>Wild Bill</u> • James Butler Hickok • Lawman • William 'Buffalo Bill' Cody • Killed cowboy Davis-Tutt in a quick-draw shootout • Shot during a poker game

<u>Clyde</u> • Clyde Barrow • Murderer, robber and kidnapper • Bonnie Parker • Masterminded a jailbreak at the Texas Department of Corrections • Ambushed

Buffalo Bill • William L. Brooks • Lawman turned outlaw • None • Became marshal of Newton, Kansas • Killed by a lynch mob before his trial

<u>Jesse James</u> • Jesse Woodson James • Bank robber • Cole Younger • Fought in the American Civil War • Shot by a gang member while dusting

<u>Wyatt Earp</u> • Wyatt Berry Stapp Earp • Lawman and saloon keeper • Doc Holliday • Involved in the gunfight at the O.K. Corral • Died of natural causes

INVENTION NO. 22
PRISON: THE GREAT ESCAPES

<u>Frank Morris</u> • Alcatraz • San Francisco, California • His attempt was made into a film, starring Clint Eastwood • 1962 • It is believed he and two others drowned in the escape, but this was never proven

<u>Jack Sheppard</u> • Newgate Prison • Central London, UK • Escaped 3 times from the same prison • 1724 • Hanged ~ friends were unable to revive him, thwarting his fourth escape attempt

Answers Page

Hey! **No cheating!**

Ronnie Biggs • Wandsworth Prison • South-west London, UK • His (brief) time in prison was for his part in the Great Train Robbery • 1965 • He spent 36 years as a fugitive but gave himself up due to ill health

Colonel Rose • Libby Prison • Richmond, Virginia • One of 109 Union prisoners to escape during the American Civil War • 1864 • Recaptured together with around half the other escapees. Later involved in a prisoner swap

Roger Bushell • Stalag Luft III • Zagan, Poland • Escaped through one of 3 tunnels named Tom, Dick and Harry • 1944 • Executed by the Nazis after being recaptured. Only 3 of the 76 escapees got to safety

Frank William Abagnale, Jr • Federal Detention Center • Atlanta, Georgia • He was a successful con artist and forger for 5 years up to the age of 21 • 1971 • He pretended to be an undercover prison inspector during his detention and bluffed his way out

Alfie 'Houdini' Hinds • Chelmsford Prison • Essex, UK • He escaped from the Old Bailey during his trial • 1957 • Recaptured and sent to serve 6 years at Parkhurst Prison

Joseph 'Whitey' Riordan • Sing Sing Prison • Ossining, New York State • One of 3 escapees in a single murderous attempt • 1941 • Executed after being recaptured using bloodhounds. One accomplice was shot dead during the escape

INVENTION NO. 23
PLASTIC SURGERY

1 – PET • Polyethylene Terephthalate: Drink bottles, plastic jars (like peanut butter jars)
2 – HDPE • High Density Polyethylene: Detergent bottles and plastic milk bottles
3 – PVC • Polyvinyl Chloride: Pipes, shrink wrap, outdoor furniture
4 – LDPE • Low Density Polyethylene: Bin bags and carrier bags
5 – PP • Polypropylene: Bottle tops and drinking straws
6 - PS • Polystyrene: Plastic cutlery, take-away boxes, foam cups

7 - OTHER • Other: Everything that doesn't fall into the other six categories

INVENTION NO. 32
CUTLERY: CUSTOMS AND ETIQUETTE

1. A. Napkin, B. Salad fork, C. Fish fork, D. Dinner fork, E. Dinner plate, F. Soup bowl, G. Dinner knife, H. Fish knife, I. Salad knife, J. Soup spoon, K. Butter knife, L. Bread plate, M. Dessert spoon, N. Dessert fork, O. Water glass. P. Red-wine glass, Q. White-wine glass

2. b / 3. a / 4. d / 5. b / 6. b / 7. a / 8. b

INVENTION NO. 38
SIGN LANGUAGE: GIVE ME A SIGN

1. d / 2. e / 3. a / 4. c / 5. b / 6. f

INVENTION NO. 39
TOILET PAPER

1. d / 2. c / 3. c / 4. c / 5. b
6. c / 7. b / 8. c / 9. c / 10. d

INVENTION NO. 46
MUSIC: WE WILL ROCK YOU

Elvis Presley • The Blue Moon Boys • 'Blue Suede Shoes' • 1950s • Rock 'n' roll • Died aged 42 from a heart attack

Freddie Mercury • Queen • 'Bohemian Rhapsody' • 1970s • Glam rock • Died aged 45 from Aids

Beyoncé Knowles • Destiny's Child • 'Crazy in Love' • 2000s • R&B • Has a successful solo career

Michael Jackson • The Jackson Five • 'Thriller' • 1980s • Pop • Career has taken a turn for the worse

Frank Sinatra • Tommy Dorsey Orchestra • 'My Way' • 1940s • Swing • Died aged 82 from a heart attack

John Lennon • The Beatles • 'She Loves You' • 1960s • Pop/rock • Died aged 40 after being shot by a fan

Answers

Answers Continued

Hey! **No cheating!**

Duke Ellington • The Washingtonians
• 'Don't Get Around Much Anymore' • 1930s
• Jazz • Died aged 75 from lung cancer

Kurt Cobain • Nirvana • 'Smells Like
Teen Spirit' • 1990s • Grunge
• Committed suicide, aged 27

INVENTION NO. 48
ASPIRIN: A QUICK FIX

1. E / 2. C / 3. B / 4. G
5. D / 6. F / 7. A

ASPIRIN: HIT THE JACKPOT!

1. Broccoli / 2. Watermelon / 3. Banana
4. Tomato / 5. Aubergine / 6. Peanut

INVENTION NO. 56
WORLD WIDE WEB:
CORRECT ROUTER

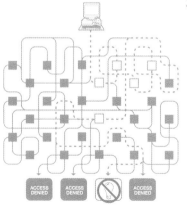

INVENTION NO. 57
CONCRETE: BUILD AND CONSTRUCT

Empire State Building • New York City, USA
• Offices • 1930–1931 • Shreve, Lamb and
Harmon Associates • The spire at the top
was originally designed as an airship mooring

Christ the Redeemer • Rio de Janeiro, Brazil
Statue • 1926–1931 • Heitor da Silva Costa
• It weighs 700 tonnes and stands 700 m
above sea level!

Eiffel Tower • Paris, France • Radio
broadcasting tower • 1887–1889 • Gustave Eiffel
• It was only supposed to stand for 20 years
and was considered an eyesore by many

The Tower • London, UK • Prison • AD 1078
onwards • William the Conqueror • Believed
to be the most haunted place in the UK

Opera House • Sydney, Australia • Music venue
• 1957–1973 • Jorn Utzon • The building design
is based on the segments of an orange

The Great Wall • China • To keep invaders out
• 221 BC onwards • Qin Shi Huang • Known
as the world's longest graveyard due to the
number of dead workers buried alongside it

The Colosseum • Rome, Italy
• Gladiator arena • AD 70–82
• Emperor Vespasian • Could be entirely
flooded so mock sea battles could be staged

Petra • Jordan • A city of tombs and temples
• 9 BC–AD 70 • Unknown • The entire site
is carved out of rock inside a canyon

Concrete used in: Empire State Building,
Christ the Redeemer Statue, Eiffel Tower,
Sydney Opera House and the Colosseum

INVENTION NO. 64
UMBRELLA: RAIN, RAIN, GO AWAY

1. b / 2. d / 3. d / 4. c
5. c / 6. b / 7. b / 8. a / 9. c

Answers Continued

Hey! **No cheating!**

INVENTION NO. 71
NUMBERS: SUDOKU

PUZZLE 1

1	3	7	5	6	9	8	4	2
6	2	5	1	4	8	3	9	7
9	4	8	7	2	3	1	6	5
7	8	3	6	9	2	4	5	1
4	1	9	3	8	5	7	2	6
2	5	6	4	7	1	9	8	3
3	7	2	8	5	4	6	1	9
5	6	4	9	1	7	2	3	8
8	9	1	2	3	6	5	7	4

PUZZLE 2

5	9	3	8	7	1	2	4	6
7	6	2	9	4	3	5	8	1
8	4	1	2	5	6	9	7	3
1	7	6	5	3	9	8	2	4
3	8	5	4	6	2	1	9	7
9	2	4	1	8	7	3	6	5
2	3	9	6	1	4	7	5	8
6	5	7	3	9	8	4	1	2
4	1	8	7	2	5	6	3	9

PUZZLE 3

6	8	4	1	2	5	3	7	9
2	9	5	7	4	3	8	6	1
3	7	1	9	8	6	4	2	5
1	2	3	8	6	4	9	5	7
4	5	7	2	3	9	1	8	6
8	6	9	5	1	7	2	4	3
5	1	8	3	7	2	6	9	4
9	4	2	6	5	1	7	3	8
7	3	6	4	9	8	5	1	2

INVENTION NO. 73
SUNSCREEN: HERE COMES THE SUN

1. b / 2. d / 3. c / 4. b / 5. d
6. b / 7. d / 8. c / 9. d / 10. d

INVENTION NO. 78
LANGUAGE DECODER: ¿USTED ENTIENDE?

1. Spanish • I love my mum •

2. Chinese • I lost my pet cat yesterday •

3. German • My teacher is an alien •

4. Hungarian • I don't speak Hungarian •

INVENTION NO. 79
TOOTHPASTE: OPEN WIDE!

1. d / 2. f / 3. c / 4. h / 5. g / 6. a / 7. e / 8. b

INVENTION NO. 80
SILK: YOU WORM!

1. d / 2. d / 3. d / 4. c / 5. d
6. b / 7. d / 8. c / 9. a / 10. d

INVENTION NO. 81
LASER: LASER BRAIN

1. CONSTRUCTION / 2. PRINTING
3. HEALTH / 4. SPACE / 5. SHOPPING
6. WAR / 7. ENTERTAINMENT

INVENTION NO. 96
KNOW-IT-ALL HAT

1. Laika, a dog
2. When they got wet, the cards peeled
apart to reveal maps and escape routes
3. 687 days / 4. Monsieur Mangetout
5. Furniture dealer / 6. Orange
7. 'I don't know' or 'I don't understand you'
8. Purple or white
9. They were code-named 'water tanks' during
the First World War to conceal their purpose
10. 206 / 11. Thigh bone / 12. Shaking hands
13. Teeth can't repair themselves
14. 19.91 seconds / 15. 14,718

INVENTION NO. 97
ALCOHOLIC DRINKS: DRUNK AS A SKUNK

1. b / 2. d / 3. d / 4. e
5. b / 6. c / 7. c / 8. c / 9. b

How to Use Your Pocket-Sized Checklist

Use the following instructions to keep track of the **Inventions**
you've mastered and pass on your knowledge at a moment's notice

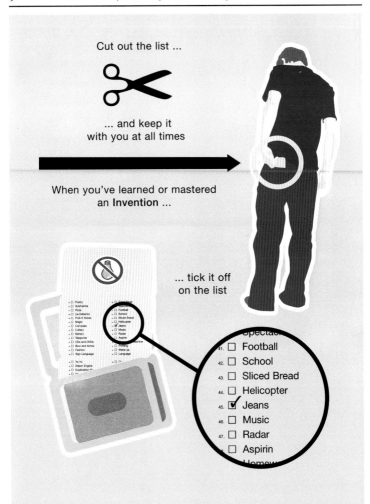

Cut out the list ...

... and keep it
with you at all times

When you've learned or mastered
an **Invention** ...

... tick it off
on the list

41. ☐ Football
42. ☐ School
43. ☐ Sliced Bread
44. ☐ Helicopter
45. ☑ Jeans
46. ☐ Music
47. ☐ Radar
48. ☐ Aspirin

Small print: Keep this list with you at all times. Use every opportunity to master the **Inventions** facts in this book and pass on your new-found knowledge.

— Fold —

☐ 1 Time	☐ 13 Satellite
☐ 2 Mobile Phone	☐ 14 Playing Cards
☐ 3 Matches	☐ 15 Tattoo
☐ 4 Cloning	☐ 16 Pencil
☐ 5 Fast Food	☐ 17 Morse Code
☐ 6 Photography	☐ 18 Fizzy Drinks
☐ 7 Time Zones	☐ 19 Birthdays
☐ 8 Nuclear Weapons	☐ 20 Thermometer
☐ 9 Money	☐ 21 Guitar
☐ 10 Time Machine	☐ 22 Prison
☐ 11 Fingerprinting	☐ 23 Plastic
☐ 12 Dynamite	☐ 24 Hot-Air Balloon

Checklist

25. ☐ Poetry
26. ☐ Submarine
27. ☐ Pizza
28. ☐ Lie Detector
29. ☐ Post-It Notes
30. ☐ Magic
31. ☐ Compass
32. ☐ Cutlery
33. ☐ Battery
34. ☐ Teleporter
35. ☐ CDs and DVDs
36. ☐ Bow and Arrow
37. ☐ Fashion
38. ☐ Sign Language

39. ☐ Toilets and Toilet Paper
40. ☐ Spectacles
41. ☐ Football
42. ☐ School
43. ☐ Sliced Bread
44. ☐ Helicopter
45. ☐ Jeans
46. ☐ Music
47. ☐ Radar
48. ☐ Aspirin
49. ☐ Homework Machine
50. ☐ Printing
51. ☐ Make-up
52. ☐ Language

53. ☐ Yo-yo
54. ☐ Steam Engine
55. ☐ Duplication Machine
56. ☐ World Wide Web
57. ☐ Concrete
58. ☐ Roller Coaster
59. ☐ Glass
60. ☐ Inter-Stellar Travel
61. ☐ Microscope and Telescope
62. ☐ Bling
63. ☐ Anaesthetics
64. ☐ Umbrella

65. ☐ Gunpowder
66. ☐ Tea
67. ☐ Dancing
68. ☐ Refrigerator
69. ☐ Weather Machine
70. ☐ Fireworks
71. ☐ Numbers
72. ☐ X-ray
73. ☐ Sunscreen
74. ☐ Braille
75. ☐ Teenagers
76. ☐ Intelligent Robots
77. ☐ Banana Suitcase

78. ☐ Language Decoder
79. ☐ Toothpaste
80. ☐ Silk
81. ☐ Laser
82. ☐ Skateboard
83. ☐ Parachute
84. ☐ Anti-Ageing Pills
85. ☐ Mirror
86. ☐ Tin-Opener
87. ☐ Passport
88. ☐ Computer
89. ☐ Barcodes

90. ☐ Maps
91. ☐ Antibiotics
92. ☐ Vinyl Records
93. ☐ Ejector Seat
94. ☐ Flip Flops
95. ☐ Soap
96. ☐ Know-It-All Hat
97. ☐ Alcoholic Drinks
98. ☐ Terraforming
99. ☐ Sticky Tape and Blu-tack
100. ☐ Chindogu
101. ☐ Room 101